THE NEW
EVANGELISM

activities are all important, but nothing can substitute for the communication of the reality of the God-experience. To care for people is to yearn that they shall, amid the loneliness of mass society, come to an encounter with the eternal. The Christian must passionately yearn to communicate the wonder of the reality of God to all who do not know him.

To offer Jesus Christ as Liberator is a motive for mission. The world cries out for deliverance in two ways: release from inner, personal bondage and release from outer oppression. Inner, compulsive habits are the scourge of today's world. Millions are living in bondage to gluttony, to alcohol, to sex, to drugs. These things cripple lives. For countless people there is a desperate need to be free within.

Jesus is a personal Savior from sin and from the consequences of sin. He sets the prisoner free. Through repentance, forgiveness, and the power of the Holy Spirit, a new life of personal liberty becomes possible. Still the great promise of the New Testament is true: "If the Son makes you free you will be free indeed" (John 8:36).

The redemption of society is a motive that throbs strongly in the mind of many Christians. Millions of people are being crushed by poverty, racial injustice, political oppression, and war. In today's mass society, many are forced to live crippled, unfulfilled lives because of the nature of urban life. Over all the world hangs the threat of pollution of the good earth, and in the background there ever stands the possible holocaust of nuclear warfare and destruction. I confess the motive for the redemption of society throbs strongly in my own mind and conscience.

There is an eschatological motive which can throb through the new evangelism. It will be different from the past, but it will be there. In early periods, the eschatological moment was cast beyond time. Living was seen in the context of the imminent return of Jesus: the so-called second coming of Christ. Now the eschatological hope can be seen as part of contemporary time. Dr. John Knox, commenting on Christ's word in the twelfth chapter of Luke, says: "All eschatological pictures are in essence attempts at dramatizing a continuing and awful fact of human life; our actions, whether good or evil, have an ultimate significance and effect of infinite range and scope. Man stands each day and hour on the verge of either hell or heaven, of either utter and final defeat or utter and final victory. This is the glory and the peculiar torment of human living."

There are times when this truth comes into personal lives. Facing some situation the challenge to accept the Christian position is a call to an eschatological decision. No decision we ever make can have more far-reaching consequences than to answer the biblical question: "What shall I do with Jesus who is called Christ" (Matt. 27:22). To be used by God to bring men and women to Christian acceptance, to release the power of Christ into human lives is greatly to bless all who come to decision. This provides a powerful motive for mission.

A new motive for mission must surely rest on obedience. To be a Christian is to be sensitive to the mind and purpose of Jesus Christ. It is to be obedient to his will.

There is no doubt that Jesus Christ summoned his followers to be his witnesses and to carry his message

14

to all people and to the ends of the earth. We hear this call in the great words following his resurrection. To his disciples he said, "Go into all the world and preach the gospel to the whole creation" (Mark 16:15). On the mount of Transfiguration his summons was just as insistent: "You shall be my witnesses in Jerusalem and all Judea, and Samaria and to the end of the earth" (Acts 1:8).

Perhaps the most moving of Christ's calls to mission is when he said in his great high-priestly prayer: "As thou didst send me into the world, so I have sent them" (John 17:18). Dr. Bruce Kendrich, in his book, *The New Humanity* (London: Collins, 1958), movingly presents this challenge and this motive: "Jesus said, As the Father has sent me, so send I you. He had been sent to identify Himself unreservedly with men, their griefs, their sufferings, to penetrate to the depth of their lives, to be wounded, to bleed, to die. That was how the Father sent Him. Now; send I you" (p. 85).

THE ARENA FOR MISSION

We live in a pre-Christian world. This is a fundamental assumption for all who as Christians would witness to Jesus Christ in an era of world mission.

If there is any phrase I find hard to accept, it is that this is a post-Christian world. This obviously raises the question: When was the world Christian? Was it Christian in the first or the tenth, the sixteenth or the nineteenth century? To ask the question is to see how absurd it is. As always, the world today awaits the full light of the Christian gospel; it is still a pre-Christian world.

What are the characteristics of this pre-Christian world? Which features must be noted in the arena into which the message of Christian mission must be thrust? Somehow a measure of the task, an estimation of the ground over which the struggle is to be waged, must be gauged.

A CITY CIVILIZATION

World civilization is increasingly a city civilization. In the year 1800, only 2 percent of the people lived in cities with a population over 100,000. By 1960 the figure was

16

35 percent; by the end of the century it will be 60 percent. Nothing seemingly can stop the growth of cities. For good or ill, the majority of the human family will have to learn how to live in cities.

There are two recent writers who present very differing pictures of city life. Dr. Harvey Cox sings the praises of the city in his book *The Secular City*. Dr. Jacques Ellul presents the city in darker hues in his book *The Meaning of the City* (Grand Rapids, Mich.: Wm. B. Eerdmans Publishing Company, 1970).

In *The Secular City* Harvey Cox celebrates the liberties and privileges of city living. In the great metropolitan areas of the world, culture is able to develop. In the cities there can be found variety and excitement, the possibility of alternate life-styles, and growing affluence. In large cities, while many are lonely, others appear to want to live detached, uninvolved, anonymous lives. People are free to choose their own friends, their own way of life. All the evidence suggests that most people, in spite of the problems of city living, long to spend their days crowded together in cities.

Jacques Ellul gives a less favorable picture of city life. He looks at the city from the perspective of the Bible. He discovers that it was Cain, the murderer of Abel, who is credited with being the founder of the city. He quotes Genesis 4:16-17: "Cain went away from the presence of the Lord, and dwelt in the land of Nod, east of Eden. Cain knew his wife, and she conceived and bore Enoch; and he built a city, and called the name of the city after the name of his son, Enoch."

Dr. Ellul accepts the city, but sees it as Cain's city. Because it is Cain's city, it cries out for redemption. He

17

says that "the city is a place where man's triumphant march without God can take place, and it is because of this triumphant march that the city is a necessity" (p. 16). Cain built a city, claims Ellul, because he was a fugitive and a wanderer. He had murdered his brother Abel and became aware of his alienation from God. Somehow, somewhere, he had to find a substitute security and a substitute companionship. So he built a city. In that city he found security and companionship amid the mass of people. So a city became a substitute both for the security found in the presence of God and for the companionship which comes from a sense of the presence of God.

No one can spend a lifetime working within the boundaries of a city, as I have, without knowing both the satisfaction and the sorrows of the city. For me the burden of city living is seen at every turn. A dominant characteristic of city life is its impersonal, uncaring spirit. People jostle each other in the crowd, and though physically near, their spirits remain far apart.

Apartment living is expanding all over the world. The world of cities is beginning to look like Moscow, where there is scarcely a house in sight. In high-rise apartment buildings, people appear almost as if they are poked into human filing cabinets elevated into the sky. In them there is little fellowship and less community living. People become like the sand on an Australian beach. Sydney's yellow beaches were created by disintegrated pieces of Hawkesbury sandstone. The grains of sand touch, but they are no longer related in some pattern as they once were in the rocks of the Hawkesbury mountains and hills. It was the unrelated life of city dwellers which led the poet Shelley to say that "hell is a city much like London."

The pace and pressure of city living place a strange burden on the human spirit. John Buchan once wrote, "The time will come when life will be lived in the glare of neon lights, and the human spirit will know no solitude." That moment has come for millions.

The nature of city life makes it hard to hear the still, small voice of God. Hence the Christian church finds it hardest to endure in the inner belts of large cities. During this century Protestantism has suffered many a retreat as it has deserted poverty-stricken inner-city areas for the more affluent suburbs. In Australia the Roman Catholic spokesman, Mr. B. A. Santamaria, says: "For every two Catholics who move from the country to the city, one is lost to the Church."

The future of civilization depends on what happens in cities. Here the decision-makers live, here life-styles develop, here are focused the influences which condition the life of people. Therefore if the Christian church is defeated in its mission within cities it suffers a crucial setback. No victory elsewhere can compensate for failure in the city.

THE WORLD OF SCIENCE

It is a truism to call this an age of science. For more than a century the advance of science has been a determining, dominant feature of the culture of the world. However, a subtle change is coming over the scene. In many ways the human family is moving into a post-scientific era. People today are less dazzled by science

19

than at any time in the history of scientific discovery and achievement. There is of course everywhere a recognition of what science has done. The conquest of nature, the insights of psychology and psychiatry, the penetration of the lair of the atom, the astonishing achievement of men stepping onto the moon, have left mankind almost spellbound.

Today some reassessment is occurring. There is a growing realization of the limitations of science. No longer do people stand in awe of space adventure. Discovery has come with such rapidity that the human mind is satiated. Dr. Leonard Griffith, in his book *Barriers to Christian Belief* (London: Hodder & Stoughton, 1961), has caught the new mood when he says: "Nothing has been found up there that has changed the ground rules down here. Nothing has been gleaned along the Milky Way which has made the good life easier or the wrong less attractive. There is nothing out there that can warm one heart chilled with loneliness here or bandage one mind that is bleeding to death from doubt, or forgive one sin that has turned one soul prematurely gray" (p. 65).

There was an incident in my early ministry which I have never been able to forget. One night after midnight, in the Australian coal-mining town where I lived, the telephone rang. There had been an accident in one of the pits. A number of men were dead. One young man, the only son of aged parents who were members of the church, was critically injured. I was asked to bring the parents to the hospital quickly. On entering the dim ward, a doctor came from behind a screened bed and drew me to one side. He told me the young man was dying. Then he added, "I can do no more, you must take over now." So I went to the bedside and tried to say something to the dying man and then turned to speak to the stricken mother and father.

That doctor's comment has always seemed to me to be symbolic. He represented the highest skill of medical science. However, he came to the moment where he had to turn to somebody of a quite different discipline, a Christian minister.

Today it is dawning on millions of people that science is morally neutral. Of itself it can create no brave, new world. It is capable of bringing great blessings to the human race. It is just as capable of bringing great cursing to people everywhere. Whether it will build or destroy will be determined outside its own research and discipline. From some other source must come power and direction if science is to lead toward peace and progress rather than war and destruction.

The Cult of Violence

The world today is a violent world. Life has become very expendable in the arena of the twentieth century. The world seems to stagger from one outbreak of violence to another.

Think of recent happenings. The murders at the Olympics, the practice of torture by so-called civilized states, the awful carnage of Northern Ireland, the unbelievable tragedy of Vietnam, the holding and slaughter of children as hostages, the hijacking of planes. So grows the mountain of sorrow created by man's inhumanity to man.

What is the cause? I believe there is a link between

21

violence in entertainment and heartlessness and sadism in real life. In ancient Rome cruel spectator sports choked the wells of pity and coarsened the souls of people. I indict the sickening violence of modern entertainment (such as in "R" films in Australia and "X" films in America) as a major cause of the growth of violence. The endless torture and destruction of living human beings presented with all the power of realistic, close-up photography is having its effects.

There is presentation of false values in current entertainment which must be eroding human standards of respect. There has always been violence in films, but in the older films the good guys always came out on top. The appalling fact about a film like *The Godfather* is that it holds up a ruthless criminal for sympathy, even for admiration. Is it any wonder that violence in fantasy becomes violence in fact? Violence has subtly become an accepted part of the way of life. There is a complete disregard of the truth of the Bible: "As a man thinketh in his heart, so is he" (Prov. 23:7 KJV).

The endless presentation of violence is having two effects. First, people with psychiatric weaknesses are being stimulated, propelled into acts of violence. Second, when the destruction of human life loses its horror, a vital and natural restraint disappears.

There are other causes. Hidden violence causes overt acts of violence. To starve people is violent; to oppress people politically is violent; to rob people of dignity and self-respect is violent. Law and order, when founded on injustice, is violent.

The murder by the Arabs of athletes from Israel at the Munich Olympic Games illustrates the truth that in-

22

justice breeds violence. Behind a dastardly crime lay the indefensible treatment by Israel and the Great Powers of the Arab refugees. Since 1948 almost a million people, swollen by a further 30,000 from the 1967 Six Days War, have been forced to live under intolerable conditions. As the World Council of Churches has said: "In supporting the establishment of the state of Israel without protecting the rights of the Palestinians, injustice has been done to the Palestinian Arabs which should be redressed."

I have visited the Arab refugee camps in Jordan. I can only say they defy description. It is an unrelieved tragedy that in order to provide a resting place for over one millions Jews harried and persecuted in Europe, another million refugees were created. So the judgments of a Dom Helder of Brazil are vividly illustrated. He has stated: "Governments must get to the root of evil and attack injustice, which is the origin of all kinds of violence."

Above all, there has been the violence of war. In this war-drenched century more human beings have died in wars than in all the centuries of recorded history put together. I do not think you can kill a man anywhere, be it at the end of hangman's rope or at the receiving end of a bayonet or bullet, without cheapening life everywhere. So the destruction of life has lost its horror, and violence has become an almost accepted feature of world life.

MORAL PERMISSIVENESS

Moral permissiveness is a feature of the arena for mission. Moral permissiveness is the name for an immoral

23

hedonism which is steadily breaking down the delicate restraints which operate between men and women; and it is leading to a corruption of the sex instinct. This represents great peril for the human family, for I would accept the statement of Cannon Raven: "Sex standards and civilization rise and fall together."

Moral permissiveness rests on the belief that there is no abiding moral authority. All is relative. The novelist Ernest Hemingway defined it well. "What is moral is what you feel good after. What is evil is what you feel bad after." It is as old as Adam and Eve. Adam and Eve tried to write their own rules and lost Paradise.

What has given rise to moral permissiveness as the 1960s advanced? In part it is a reaction against Victorian hypocrisy. It is a delayed consequence of World War II. It is the reflection of the new freedom in man-woman relationships which has come with the control of the sex function, with birth control pills. In a way it represents people's inability to handle a vast, new freedom; and as a result freedom has become confused with license. It is greatly furthered by the power of mass media. It is the moral or immoral consequences of the decline of religious faith and practice. As Dr. W. E. Sangster once claimed: "Morality does not survive its severance from religious sanctions for more than two generations."

There are undoubted gains which have come with a more flexible approach to moral issues. The openness and frankness of the discussion which now surrounds sexual matters is healthy. On the other hand, because of this generation's inability to handle a new freedom, a new moral maturity will probably develop. There has come

24

with it a new liberation of women. For the first time some equality in many intimate areas of human living is emerging.

However, on balance, moral permissiveness has so far brought more cursing than blessing. Moral permissiveness is based on two basic distortions of the truth. First, moral permissiveness puts the satisfactions of life within the life and the body of the individual. So reach for alcohol or a chemical drug that release may come, that heightened perception, an enrichment of inner satisfaction be gained. So plunge into unrestricted sex, treat it just for fun, satisfy the cravings of the instincts and live. This is a highway to self-centeredness and irresponsibility. To weaken Poland, Hitler subverted the land by sending in a flood of pornographic material. His assumption was that if he could get people absorbed in their own bodily sensations, they would care less about what may be happening around them. True life does not lie in plunging into the ego, but in looking beyond it; by having heads lifted from the trough, not buried in it. Second, moral permissiveness leads straight to a new bondage. The very beginning of civilization is the conquest of basic self-centered urges and desires. Human maturity means being master of the self, holding under control and in balance the thrusts and drives of desire. To accept the thesis that to want to do something is justification for doing it is in the end to become a slave to imperious desire.

There is no advancement in encouraging in the name of freedom such developments as pornography. Pornography is but the organization of lust on a large scale and the prelude to inner tyranny. There is no roadway to freedom by abortion on demand or temporary marriage or

premarital or extramarital sex. This is the highway not to
freedom but to bondage. Moral permissiveness represents
the exploitation of the people. Women, actors and
actresses are under threat through growing permissiveness
of a new and growing form of exploitation.

During and since the nineteenth century, we have
learned that moral permissiveness brings suffering and
sorrow to the people. The nineteenth century was thor-
oughly permissive toward economic evils. Governments
only slowly awakened to the evils of early industrializa-
tion, to the perils of colonialism. By exercising no restraints, by allowing men and women to do as they
pleased, a period of tragic exploitation, of long working
hours in pits and factories, and of conquered peoples in
primitive countries overseas came to the Western world.

Today, in economic and political matters, society has
rejected permissiveness. Society is hedged with all manner of controls aimed at stopping the exploitation of
one man by another, of society by groups, and powerful
interests ready to put profits before the welfare of people.
On the question of pollution, society is in the process
of completely rejecting permissiveness, substituting for it
rigid controls over man's greed and irresponsibility.

It is strange that at this time voices are raised calling
for all controls to disappear in areas such as pornography.
Why this cannot be seen as opening the floodgates of
exploitation is beyond my comprehension.

Moral permissiveness represents the exploitation of at
least half the human family, women. The purchase of
women's bodies for public display by the magazine and
film industry is one of the ugliest features of modern
society. It reaches its height in streets of prostitution

in cities like Frankfurt and Hamburg where women on display in windows are selected by men, much as a carcass of mutton is chosen in an Australian butcher's shop.

The woman always pays, it is said; and womanhood is certainly paying a price, the price of exploitation under today's moral permissiveness.

THE PRIMACY OF ECONOMIC ISSUES

For the next twenty years mankind will probably be concentrating on world economic problems. For most of humanity, it will be a case of facing the stark reality of survival. In the West the days of easy affluence are over. A crisis of terrifying proportions cannot be far away.

The visit of the former President Nixon to China marked the end of an era. Since the rise of Hitler in the 1930s, the focus has been on international affairs. Following World War II there was in the Western world a pathological spirit of anticommunism. Over all the earth hung the threat of atomic destruction. For almost forty years the major concentration of human effort has been directed to the solving of international tensions and overcoming the threat of war.

One result of the mood of these years has been the neglect of a search for economic progress. The fear of communism has stifled ordered reform and has resulted in a perpetuation of injustice in the economic ordering of society. Now that neglect is catching up with the world. Now the economic structure of society is beginning to creak and groan and is unable to carry the strain being placed on it. Now suffering multiplies because of a failure to find greater equality and justice in the distribution of the economic resources of the earth.

The worldwide problem of inflation is basically caused by the population explosion outstripping available food and energy resources. The vastly expanded human family is competing for insufficient resources. Inflation is a vivid and clear warning of deepening troubles to come. The gulf between those who have and those who have not is widening. In spite of the drive for increased production in places like India, the multiplication of people is canceling out any gains from planned economic development. The demand of affluent nations to go on increasing affluence is an immoral cornering of available world resources. Therefore within nations and between nations the conflict between the few with much and the many with little becomes even more critical.

The sudden emergence of the ecological crisis is forcing a whole new assessment of economic realities. For years the way in which responsible people in the affluent West have faced the poverty of the rest of the earth has been to struggle through development programs and international aid, to lift backward peoples toward the standards of living which have become accepted in the so-called advanced nations. Now it is suddenly realized that if the rest of the world does move toward Western-style affluence and wastefulness, this planet will be exhausted in a short period of time. There is no way around it if the whole world demands an ever rising gross national product and unrestricted affluence. This now appears to be a recipe for disaster.

Jesus began his ministry at Nazareth, showing he was conscious of the needs of the poor. He said, "The Spirit of the Lord is upon me, because he has anointed me to preach good news to the poor" (Luke 4:18). An awareness of the poor is a prerequisite for effective evangelism in today's world. The South American theologian Father Gutierrez in his book, *Theology of Liberation* (New York: Orbis Books, 1973), shows why poverty is so great an offence to God and man. "Poverty," he says, "represents a sundering both of solidarity among men and also of communion with God. Poverty is an expression of a sin, that is, of a negation of love. It is therefore incompatible with the coming of the Kingdom of God, a Kingdom of love and justice" (p. 295).

In this hour the Christain church faces heavy responsibilities. There is an urgent need in the Western world for a Christian critique of capitalism, and Christian thinking has been almost silent on the economic structure of society. Yet to speak with a prophetic voice in economic terms poses great difficulty. It will be more controversial for the church and its pulpits to come to grips with the injustices of the economic order than to confront international realities, such as the iniquity of the Vietnam War.

Yet in the arena for mission, economic issues in coming days cannot be avoided. If the church fails to proclaim the Kingdom of God in economic terms, it will betray its Lord and abandon the people. Perhaps only the church with its influence amid the middle-class masses of the people can prepare the mind of the people for inevitable change. The alternative to prophetic grappling with the economic structure of society by the church could be endless world upheavel and the tragic denial of a high quality of economic justice for all people.

FUTURE SHOCK

When Alvin Toffler wrote his now famous book *Future Shock*, he uncovered one of the undeniable features of today's world. The impact of rapid social change on the mind, the emotions, and the patterns of life is undoubtedly tremendous. Who does not at times feel like he is on an escalator gone crazy? The speed of change throws us all off balance. Since 1940 the world has seen the advent of color television, atomic power, manmade fibers, heart transplants, antibiotic drugs, polio vaccine, jet airplanes, computers, artificial satellites, instant communication, and walking on the moon.

Take the growth of knowledge alone. It took from the first year of the Christian era to 1750 for knowledge to double, then from 1750 to 1900 it doubled again, then from 1900 to 1950 it doubled once more. Now, it has taken only twenty years from 1950 to 1970 to double once again. How does anybody keep pace with this growth of knowledge? No wonder Dr. Margaret Mead says that "everybody over thirty years of age is a migrant in today's world."

Recently in Australia I shared in a television series entitled "World Shapers." It sought to deal with human reactions to the elements which make for future shock. In successive television programs we tried to interpret women's liberation, the effect of chemicals on character, death control, life control through genetic engineering, the consequence of mass tenement living, the future of freedom, the significance of the world becoming a global village, the growing problems of leisure, ecology and the threat of pollution, and the future of God himself.

If life is to be lived adequately, there must be present the two elements of continuity and change. When either develops at the expense of the other and a balanced relationship between these two vital aspects is lost, millions of people cannot cope with existence. This is what is happening to many people around us today, and especially to the older segments of society. Confusion, bewilderment, retreat from living, and despair are being strengthened.

The Christian faith has a double role to play. It must not look backward. If it allies itself with the nostalgic mood of today, it will have little leadership to offer. On the other hand, the church must not shut its eyes to the need to provide security through becoming one of the continuing factors in society. The church has a vital function to see that gains of yesterday are carried into tomorrow. Everything that is new is not necessarily good, and everything that is old is not necessarily bad. The church is society's oldest and most experienced institution and can greatly serve this generation by sometimes being conservatively prophetic and by trying to make sure that values and standards and insights discovered yesterday and today are not lost for future generations. The Christian church makes a great contribution to the lives of people as it teaches them to sing such Christian songs as,

> In heavenly love abiding,
> No change my heart shall fear

> and

> Change and decay in all around I see;
> O thou who changest not, abide with me.

31

The Religious Scene

What does the religious map of the world look like in this last quarter of the twentieth century? It is a contrasting scene. To look in one direction is to see retreat and decline, yet to peer into other parts of the world is to see advance and confidence.

In older parts of the earth where Christendom was once strong, the picture is bleak. The church is suffering serious decline in countries such as Sweden, Germany, and England. Few people go to church in Scandanavia or London. The British scene is depressing with agnosticism in the ascendency, particularly in mass media, and thousands of churches struggling for survival. The loss of Christian morale in England is startling. Perhaps the loss of religious virility is a reflection of national decline and the eclipse of Britain as a world power. Whatever the cause, the passing of England as a major religious force in the world represents great loss to the human family.

A contrasting picture of growth and confidence can be seen in Africa, in Indonesia, in South America and, if all the years of this century are examined, in the United States of America. It is obvious that while the old geographic area of Christendom which once stretched from Russia to the Mediterranean is breaking up, a new Christendom unrelated to geography is emerging. This new Christendom comes from the mighty missionary movements of the last 150 years, and the growth of the church as a world force comes from the allegiance of tens of millions of new Christians.

I remember an incident at the Uppsala assembly of

the World Council of Churches. There had come to the rostrum several speakers from Europe and America who had expressed despondency and negativism which was all too typical of the late sixties. They were followed by a small figure representing the National Council of Churches in Indonesia. He said simply, "I do not know why so doleful a picture of the church is being given. In my country so many people are clamoring to enter the Christian church that we do not know how quickly enough to prepare them for baptism or how adequately to receive them into the Christian fellowship."

Let us face it, during the 1960s the world faced a serious spiritual depression, possibly the worst for two hundred years. In the days of John Wesley a mood of defeatism developed. Bishop Butler who lived in that period was once asked who he thought might be his successor, his reply being that he questioned whether there would need to be one, for he doubted whether the church would survive his own lifetime. This kind of doleful prophecy has often been heard in recent years, confusing the laity and encouraging those beyond the church who despised its witness to redouble their attacks upon it.

All issued in the absurd currency given to the phrase "death of God," Dr. Jacques Ellul gives the ironic answer such faithlessness deserved: "You thought you had killed God? Really? Because your techniques allow you to go faster than sound? Because uranium has enabled you to measure the age of the world? Because you observe that you can make matter disappear in your machines faster than sand through your fingers? Because you burst the atom and can now annihilate the earth? Because your police methods can arrest anybody, anywhere? And

33

in all that, you say, you nowhere saw God. The God who is dead is the one you made up for yourselves, and not the One who has created you" (p. 175).

Thank God this period of despondency is rapidly passing. People everywhere are seeing how false this period was; as Dr. Scott McPheat of Australia has said: "Christians have been overexposed to the world and underexposed to the gospel." Events are throwing up much evidence of what the world begins to look like when God is banished from its life. God himself is breaking through with new life into the minds and hearts of people and into their corporate religious institutions. The gospel of Jesus, with a rediscovered attractiveness, stands appealingly before the youth of the world. Sociological developments are showing how relevant the Christian church is set amid a lonely mass society. Amid the corruptions of political power the church stands with new stature against the loss of integrity in many other institutions of society. So a new confidence is arising among Christians and in the Christian church in the unending mission of Jesus in today's world.

Spiritual hunger and cries for transcendence are heard among masses of people. In the Western world, millions are realizing that people cannot live by science or affluence alone. No meaning for existence arises out of matter. Unless something comes from beyond that which is visible, the visible world is meaningless. So gropingly, in some cases in mistaken ways, people of all ages are crying out for the eternal.

The cry for God can be heard in the interest in transcendental meditation and in eastern religions. There is the emergence of the Jesus movement, with young people seeking through religion a satisfaction which they falsely sought elsewhere, such as through drugs.

The rise of the occult and the resurgence of magic and witchcraft are strange phenomena. Yet, are they? The alternative to religious faith is never materialism or agnosticism, but superstition. When Saul, King of Israel, no longer had his heart turned toward God, he took the sad journey to the witches' cave at Endor. Having lost his hold on God (or more accurately, having blinded himself to God's hold on him), he sought satisfaction elsewhere—in his case, in the superstitious belief in the witches cavern. Many today are taking the same road to Endor, and they are doomed to find the same disappointment Saul found.

Aldous Huxley once said: "There is a God-shaped blank in modern man's heart." That emptiness is becoming more apparent. If there is a God-shaped blank in the human soul, only the shape of God can fill it.

Among Christians there is a heightened yearning for what may be called the God-experience. Millions are turning inward, seeking satisfying religious experience, as in the Pentecostal movement and in the spiritual-growth movements in churches. A growing hunger for God is a sign of the times.

The protest era seemingly has passed. Youth is no longer excited by causes. Ideologies are dead. People are today marching for nothing and for nobody. They are no longer at the rostrum carrying banners. I mourn the passing of the protest movement of the sixties. Many Christians took a worthy part in the struggle against racism, oppression, and war. Something very vital is dying in the life of the church and the country.

No survey of today's religious scene would be complete

without a recognition of the tremendous significance of the ecumenical movement. The establishment of the World Council of Churches at Amsterdam in 1948 was one of the truly historic events of the twentieth century. Drawing together the Protestant and Orthodox churches, east and west, young and old, it inaugurated a new Christian era. Then came Pope John and the Second Vatican Council. New life surged through the ancient life of the Roman Catholic Church. Since then the miracle has happened: we have seen the crumbling of the walls of partition between Protestants and Roman Catholics. Through it all, I believe, God has been at work regrouping the followers of his Son for the next great Christian advance in history.

Perhaps the first sign of this new age is seen in another contemporary feature in the religious scene. It is a recovery in the church of a passion for mission. As yet it is in its early stages and is found only in some areas of the church's life. Yet Christians are discovering in church after church, in land after land, the truth of Emil Brunner's statement: "The church exists by mission, as a fire exists by burning."

I choose one illustration of the new concern for mission within the world Christian community. It lies behind the launching of World Mission 1975 by the World Methodist Council. At the Twelfth World Methodist Conference in Denver, Colorado, the decision was taken that the Methodist churches of the world would go on mission where possible with ecumenical participation. Some fifty-five constituent churches of the Council are prepared in concert to witness to the whole world with the gospel of Jesus Christ.

36

World Mission '75 is an expression of the concept that the era of World Mission has begun. It is a world church sharing together its resources, each part of the world helping each other part in mission. For the first time in history, a world community of churches will, for the period of a year, seek to do together what John Wesley constantly did for England in the eighteenth century: offer men and women Christ.

On November 22, 1974, the World Methodist Mission was launched. At Shepherds Field, near Bethlehem, several thousands of Christians assembled. They were very conscious that it was only a few miles away that Jesus said finally to his disciples on the day of Ascension, "You shall be my witnesses in Jerusalem, and in all Judea and Samaria and to the ends of the earth" (Acts 1:8). Many were conscious of the claim made by Dr. William Temple: "We are the early Christians." In faith and hope, recommissioned for mission, the modern followers of Jesus streamed away to the ends of the earth to do his bidding.

THE MESSAGE OF MISSION

Announce the Kingdom! This was the charge Jesus gave to his followers: "Go and proclaim the kingdom of God" (Luke 9:60).

The first task of evangelism is to find the message to be proclaimed. The effectiveness of mission depends primarily on message. Too often when thinking of evangelism, the church at once begins thinking of method, of technique. But what shall it profit a church if it perfects its techniques and has nothing to say?

The Christian message to be proclaimed varies according to place and time. While in one sense the gospel of Jesus is unchanging, it must be relevant. This means that Christians must grapple with the question: What would be God's word for this place and this hour?

I recall one experience in my own life which showed vividly how differing conditions demand a differing accent of message. In the 1950s I led the Mission to the Nation for the Methodist Church in Australia. Following this experience I was invited to undertake a similar task for the Methodist Church in America. For the first three months I preached with the emphasis which appeared effective in Australia. Somehow I felt it was failing.

The turning point came, I remember, at Colorado Springs. There one night I preached on the theme "Religion or Jesus Christ." It expressed my growing conviction that the mood was different. In the religious boom period of the 50s everybody in America, unlike Australia, seemed to believe in God. For America the real issue was in what kind of God do people believe. With this change of emphasis I believe I became more effective in evangelism in America.

Hence every preacher in his study, every theological school, must be grappling with the question: What would God have us say now? According to the effectiveness with which this question is answered, the effectiveness and relevance of mission will be determined.

The Personal and the Social

There are few greater needs in the church today than to find a synthesis between personal evangelism and social witness. Across the world, and especially in America, there is a tragic division between Christians who emphasize personal faith and piety and those who would witness to the faith in terms of social structure and world need. For decades a polarization between these two elements of the gospel has inhibited the power of Christian witness. Evangelism today bears a heavy burden because too often it has failed to fashion a Christian social conscience. There is a form of evangelism which has played a dread part in endorsing by silence and perpetuating by timidity, oppression, and evil.

Recently there has appeared a new biography of George Whitefield, the eighteenth-century preacher. Dr. Arnold

Dallimore tells the astonishing story of the popular success of Whitefield. As George Whitefield preached from place to place in the eastern states of America, the crowds that gathered were phenomenal. It is claimed 80 percent of the population of America at that time had heard him preach.

However, Whitefield was silent on the great social issue of slavery. Compromised by owning slaves he had inherited, he could say no more than that slaves should be treated kindly and justly. No prophetic word came from his lips against the iniquity of slavery as an institution. Dr. Dallimore comments: "Whitefield had the ear of the people, as no other man would have for many years. How different might have been the lot of the slaves had he fought for their liberation. America was being remolded in the fires of revival, new forces of freedom and compassion were being born, how changed might have been the history of the nation had it embarked in that early day, on a course of liberty and justice for all, black as well as white" (*George Whitefield* [London: Banner of Truth Trust, 1970], p. 509).

Whitefield failed, offering only a pious evangelism. He made a dread contribution by that failure to the ultimate civil war which overwhelmed the American nation. The scandal of pietistic religion which leaves men and women in bondage continues today. All over the world there are Christians who live faithful and good lives in terms of personal morality, but who by their silence and inactivity perpetuate wrong.

Some years ago a prominent Methodist layman in the United States in a symposium at the height of the early struggle against segregation in the southern states of

America said, "To be a Christian is to accept Jesus Christ as your Savior; because I don't want my daughter to go to school with a Negro boy, I don't see what that has to do with being a Christian."

Millions have turned from the Christian faith because of this tragic attitude. Evangelism must forever struggle on two fronts; it must seek the conversion of men and women for God and struggle to create a world in which all people are free.

On the other hand, let it be stated bluntly that social agitation which has lost touch with an evangelical base is largely beating the air. The old statement that there can not be a new world without new men and women is fundamentally true. An older evangelism neglected the bodies of men and women and overemphasized the soul, but today there is the peril of seeing people only in their physical dimension.

I heard recently of a Christian minister who became interested in ecology. He arranged a conference with all the people in the town concerned about pollution. In their enthusiasm, delegates arrived and erected signs outside the conference hall: "Save Our Water," "Save Our Air," "Save Our Forests." The conference was just commencing when suddenly through the door came a rather large woman. She carried a sign, and on it in big letters were the words "Save Our Souls." Seeing her the minister turned to the chairman of the gathering and said quietly, "As soon as I saw her I knew she was a troublemaker."

The "Affirmation on Salvation Today" which was issued by the Bangkok Conference of the World Council of Churches ties the two aspects of the one gospel together.

41

To the individual Christ comes with power to liberate him from every evil and sin, from every power in heaven and earth and from every threat of life or death.

To the world He comes as Lord of the universe with deep compassion for the poor and the hungry to liberate the powerless and the oppressed. To the powerful and the oppressors he comes in judgment and mercy.

How can the conviction that personal evangelism and social witness must belong together be expressed in the pulpit, by the church on mission? First of all, the message of evangelism must have personal and social elements of the gospel intertwined. The claim that to get a man's or a woman's heart right is to put the world right is a dangerous half truth. No mind is fashioned on questions that are never discussed. A conscience will only develop in any community of Christians on a certain issue as that issue is held up for Christian thought and discussion. The test of a church is the conscience it develops among its members on the great issues of the day.

True evangelical preaching must, in every utterance, reveal social overtones. To preach only on a social issue is to offer people a stone when they need bread. To offer religion only in personal terms is to create morally and spiritually undeveloped Christians.

The Greek concept of middle axioms is important. A middle axiom stands between a vague generalization and the detailed application of a truth to a particular problem. A Christian conscience is not sharpened by vague generalizations. On the other hand, it is not the task of the church to enter into the field of detailed solutions which must come from the specialist. An illustration from my Australian situation may help.

In Australia it is possible to talk about the brotherhood of man and to achieve little in terms of fashioning a Christian social conscience. To relate that general concept to Australia's immigration policy, to attack the so-called white-Australia policy, is to obtain an immediate reaction. This I believe the church must do. However, it is not the task of the preacher to tell the nation how many people from all races should be admitted into the country. Such questions as how many can be given employment in the work force, how many houses can be built, must be considered. This is to be determined by the government specialist.

There are times when, if social witness is to be effective, it must become more than words, it must involve overt action. Words are always cheap. Sometimes it is necessary to put our bodies where our minds and consciences may be. Nonviolent protest and demonstration in the name of the full gospel can and at times must be part of a true evangelism.

Above all, it is necessary to declare the biblical base for social witness. In the social and political witness of the great sixth-century prophets before Jesus we are shown the way. They did not speak as politically minded citizens. They spoke out of their awareness of the righteousness, the judgment, the mercy of God. So it must be in the proclamation today of a total gospel. There are great Christian principles and doctrines which give rise to a relevant social and political message. Evangelism is on firm ground when it can show that social concern rises from the theological reality of the gospel.

43

The Doctrine of God

The central message for mission today is God himself. The doctrine of God is at the heart of everything. If there is no God, obviously everything related to religion falls to the ground. On the other hand, if God exists, if he matters at all, he must matter most of all. Therefore, the first message for evangelism is the reality of God.

The short "death of God" era brought one important gain. It thrust God into the center of thought and controversy, in the church and in the world. For years God, even to the Christian, had been out of focus. Secondary doctrines of the Christian faith had gained the ascendancy. Suddenly all was changed and even the popular press found that God was news. Books like *Honest to God* by Bishop Robinson became bestsellers overnight. The existence and the nature of God became debated across the world.

The concept of the death of God was the natural and expected climax to the period through which we have lived. Deism, the belief that God exists but is far away and is unconcerned with the world he has made, had been on the ascendancy. It is a short step from living as though there were no relevant God at work in history to saying simply: There is no God. This is the point millions have reached, hence the bolder expression in society of agnosticism, of atheism, in recent years. I suggest that twenty years ago, prominent journalists would have hesitated to write as one recently did in Australia, saying with a note of pride, "I am a card-carrying atheist."

God for me is obvious, inescapable, inevitable. I see him everywhere. He is the great reality. Seeing God is like finding the solution to an old-type picture puzzle. Traced deceptively in the branches and twigs of a tree, there is the outline of a woman's face. The game is to turn that picture this way and that until that hidden face is seen. For a time nothing is there. Then suddenly the face is discovered. From that moment to look at the tree is always at once to see the hidden pattern. So, for me is God. I see him everywhere as I look at life and history and the universe.

Preaching the doctrine of God means presenting him as Creator. It is to echo the theme of St. Paul: "Ever since the creation of the world his invisible nature, namely, his eternal power and diety, has been clearly perceived in the things that have been made" (Rom. 1:20).

To the philosopher, the argument from design—the claim that the created world points to a creator—may not be convincing. But to the average man and woman it is a powerful argument. The penetration by science inward to the atom and outward into limitless space has heightened a sense of wonder at the range and intricacy and cohesion of the created universe. The emergence of the spark of life with presently rational human beings points to an intellect who planned and created it all. Even the peril ecologically of the world has deepened convictions about the fact and the wisdom of a creator. To present God as Creator is part of the task of evangelism today.

We shall proclaim the relevance of God. God is involved in history; he is no deistic abstraction. He belongs to the world of today.

God is found in the living present, the passing moment, now. God is not up there, out there, or even down there in the so-called "ground of all being." The location game is really over, God is not an object or a thing, God is not above the bright blue sky or out beyond the horizon or in the depths of our own consciousness. God is not above the bright blue sky or out beyond the mighty acts. He is wrapped up in his deeds. He is to be found in events. God's hiddenness is revealed in the happenings of creation, history, and personal experience. God protrudes into our world as judge. History is the story of the judgments of God.

Dr. Emerson Fosdick, on the fortieth anniversary of his ordination to the Christian ministry, preached a notable sermon in Riverside Church, New York. In it he said: "Such time as is now left for my ministry is dedicated to one major aim. It is to put back where it belongs the truth that there is an everlasting right to which our nation, our schools, our race relations, our churches, and our personal lives must be conformed if any salvation is to visit us." That declaration is more valid today than when it was uttered. In the moral permissiveness of the present, the world cries out for the message that there is an everlasting right.

The staggering Watergate scandal in America shows the end result of the loss of moral authority. How did it happen that President Nixon lost his way? I suggest the answer is found in his resignation speech. The former President said: "I would say only that if some of my judgments were wrong, they were made in what I believed at the time to be in the best interests of the nation." There it is. The idolatrous nation and its supposed highest interests took precedence over God's moral law. Anything, even burglary and deceit became permissible, for there was no consciousness of an everlasting right.

In the end Watergate proved to be a striking vindication of the belief that there is a moral law which cannot be flouted. As fact after fact was dragged into the light of day, the words of Jesus became startlingly relevant: "Nothing is covered that will not be revealed, or hidden that will not be known. What I tell you in the dark, utter in the light; and what you hear whispered, proclaim from the housetops" (Matt. 10:26-27). Perhaps we should say, shall be uncovered by recording tapes and be seen by the television cameras.

Sometimes I think the only message worth telling is that God is Love. In our kind of world I just want to sing, "O, the wonder of it all, to know that God loves me."

There are so many facts in today's world which make the love of God a relevant and powerful message. The vastness of the universe seems to make unimportant this small planet swimming in space. The population explosion appears to make every one of us a replaceable unit. Under the pressures of a mass society, people who live huddled in cities yearn for a sense of belonging, a belief that somebody cares.

This consequence of atheism is beginning to dawn in countless minds. A godless universe is a loveless universe. If there is nothing beyond matter then all is meaningless. As at least one atheist had the realism to say: "For us atheists nothing is promised, and no one is waiting."

Into this kind of world we can go and say: God is love—like Jesus. The "eclipse of God" is over. God not only exists but waits to enter into a living relationship with every man and woman who will trust him. Every one of us, irrespective of temperament, can share in the God-experience. No matter who we are or what we have done, God makes himself available to us. If with all your heart you truly seek him, you shall surely find him; this is the promise.

Yet there is something even beyond this we can say. God seeks us more than we seek him. Always he comes toward us, coming, not only half way, but all the way to meet us. It is God's seeking love which is ultimately the hope of us all.

> I sought the Lord, and afterward I knew
> He moved my soul to seek Him, seeking me;
> It was not I that found, O Saviour true,
> No, I was found of Thee.

Jesus Christ

Christianity is Jesus. To a degree that is true of no other world religion, the Christian faith is centered on Jesus. With the birth of Jesus, the faith began, with his teachings, his living, dying, rising again, it was shaped. From his action in calling a few men to be with him, the concept of the church was born. With the baptism of the Holy Spirit which was his promise, the church was propelled into history. Christianity is Jesus.

The world today is in the process of rediscovering Jesus. In recent years we have witnessed the astonishing event which can only be described as the modern resurrection of Jesus. Into the youth culture has come the Jesus Revolution. Songs about Jesus are second only to love songs on the hit-parades on the radio stations. Popular plays like *Godspell* and *Jesus Christ Superstar* attract millions around the world. Books flow out from the printing presses everywhere about Jesus. Jesus who has been around for two thousand years, suddenly has become the man of the year.

On the debit side of the Jesus revival are the shallowness of much thinking about him and the peril of seeing Jesus as just one of the religious leaders of history. Part of the task of evangelism now is to take the current interest in Jesus and carry it further answering the question: Who really is Jesus?

The message for mission must proclaim the uniqueness of Jesus. Christians in the West have been caught unready for the new pluralism which is resulting from direct, immediate contact with other world religions. Frequent and rapid travel, uneasiness about memories of the colonial era, and the appearance of representatives of other world religions in the so-called Christian West are resulting in uncertainty and confusion. So syncretism has reared its head again. Voices within the Christian community are heard suggesting almost that Jesus is a light instead of *the* light of the world, that one religion is as good as another.

There can be no compromise about the uniqueness of Jesus. Whenever the Christian church has faltered in its belief that Jesus is unique, it has lost its way. If Jesus is not the one name for all people, for all seasons, the universal man, then the claims of Christianity are fake. With humility and sensitivity the Christian has no alternative but to go on saying: "There is no other name given under heaven whereby men and women can be saved except through Jesus."

How shall Jesus be proclaimed? First Jesus is the unique revealer of God. As Jesus himself declared: "He who has seen me has seen the Father" (John 14:9).

49

In a radio forum in Sydney I once heard Dr. D. T. Niles give a powerful witness to the uniqueness of Jesus. A questioner asked him how he presented Jesus in Hindu and Buddhist Ceylon. Dr. Niles answered with a smile: "I just repeat the words of Jesus: 'No man comes to the Father but by me.' " He went on to explain that he did not deny that men and women could come to God by other religious leaders, but that in no other way but through Jesus can there be a coming to God as Father, to the Christian God.

The Jesus life-style is part of the message we offer today. In an hour when alternative life-styles are being considered, in the midst of a sexual revolution, there is great relevance in the Christian way of life.

The world is obviously passing through a period of much experimentation in how to live. The way of life of earlier generations is under question. I confess I did not think in my lifetime I would see a situation arise where the institution of marriage, of the rightness of one man and one woman being loyal to each other for life, would be under attack. Yet this is only one area of Christian ethics under debate.

The early name given to Christians was "followers of the way." In that first century there was a marked difference between the style of life that developed in the followers of Jesus and that which was the accepted way of life in the society of the time. Hence people living the Jesus way were presently called "people of the way." So today, as conventional morality is breaking down, the difference, the uniqueness of the Christian life-style can be more forcibly presented. Think of some of the elements of the Jesus life-style. Jesus pushed everything inward toward interior motives. He directed attention, not so much to adultery as to lusting after a woman, not only to murder but to hate for a brother that leads to murder. Inner integrity of thought and emotion were the concern of Jesus.

The pushing of self from the scene and the placing of a neighbor's interest and God's will at the center of consciousness are the Christian way. The losing of self for others sake is the radical ethic of Jesus. To become encased in self-interest is to be restricted, to live for others is to be released. The secret of living is not to do our own thing but to find and to do God's thing.

The nonviolence of Jesus is part of his new life-style. At a time when social change is urgent and necessary, Jesus offers a method of change through nonviolence which perhaps alone can save the world. In an age when human values and human decency are forever threatened by the crescendo of violence Jesus shows this different way. Jesus is the greatest exponent of nonviolence in history. It forms part of his gift to us today.

Christ crucified is the message for today. Ever since St. Paul declared that he could do no other than boast of the cross of Jesus, the crucifixion has been at the heart of the message of evangelism. There it must continue to stand today.

There is a cross which is the climax of the Jesus way of life. It is the cross of sacrifice which we are all invited to share. It is everybody's Calvary. At a time when followers of Jesus like Dietrich Bonhoeffer, Paul Schneider, and Martin Luther King have made the ultimate sacrifice, many see clearly that there is a cross which belongs to the very heart of the Christian life-style, a cross we are all asked to share.

There is another cross in the Christian story. It is the cross which belongs to Jesus alone. There was a cross which Jesus bore for us and our salvation. It is the cross which comes to grips with human sin. By dying Jesus did something for us which goes far beyond what he would have done by living. What that something is has never been adequately expressed by Christian theology. Yet the power, the magnetism of the crucifixion comes from Christ's redemptive act in dying for us.

Dr. Karl Menninger has written a striking book called *Whatever Became of Sin?* (New York: Hawthorn Books, 1973). In it he takes to task a Christian leadership which has minimized the fact and the power of sin, which has allowed sin to become either merely a crime or a sickness. As a result, he claims, the sense of moral responsibility, of being accountable for what we do has declined. As a result society has become self-indulgent, confused, flabby. And because what used to be called sin remains, people are more burdened with guilt and anxiety than ever. For where there is no sin there is no salvation.

There is "a great sin, the heart of all sin," says Dr. Menninger. "Some call it selfishness. Some call it alienation. Some call it schizophrenia. Some call it egocentricity. Some call it separation!" (p. 189).

No Christian message will be adequate today which does not come to grips with human sin. Whatever else he did Jesus came into the world, as John the Baptist said, to remove the sin of the world. And there is no one else but Jesus to do it.

One day a man with no faith wandered into a Paris

cathedral. He heard a choir singing: "O Lamb of God that takes away the sin of the world." The message arrested his mind. "O God, what a dream," he said. "Take away the sin of the world indeed—and yet—if only he could!"

He can, and he does. This is the wonder, the relevance, the power of the Christian message. Because Jesus lived and died and rose again, our sins can be forgiven, everyone of us can go free. This is the fundamental meaning of the crucifixion of Jesus.

Evangelism must present the truth that men and women are transformed, not by theories of the atonement but by the fact of the crucifixion. In New Testament days, people said simply, "Jesus died for me." This rudimentary faith was enough to set them free. So it is with us. To look on the cross of Jesus, to allow thought and life to flow out toward him in trust and gratitude is enough. Whatever later may follow in interpretation and intellectual understanding, salvation can come to us when we say that Christ died for us. No presentation of Jesus is complete without the message of resurrection. In the resurrection is the climax, the triumph of the ministry of Jesus.

There must have been a resurrection because Christ is alive now. This is the message to be proclaimed. I do not believe evangelism should show much interest in such questions as who moved the stone from Joseph's tomb where Jesus lay or the fact that the grave was empty, or what happened to the body of Jesus. The resurrection rests on one far more fundamental fact. There must have been a resurrection because Christ is forever alive.

The power of the resurrection comes from the living

Christ. Dr. Vincent Taylor claims: "The very basis of the New Testament experience was a faith-union between Jesus as a leader and the people who gathered around him." The significance of the resurrection is that death did not disturb this relationship. There remains for the Christian today, for all who will place their trust in Jesus Christ, a faith-union which nothing can destroy.

THE DOCTRINE OF THE HOLY SPIRIT

An understanding of the doctrine of the Holy Spirit is essential to evangelism today. If God is to be relevant, he must be seen at work in human lives, in the church, and in history. God is in action today, this is what the doctrine of the Holy Spirit is asserting.

There is a Spirit at work in the world who is always trying to lead people out of bondage into freedom, desiring that every human being should find true fulfillment. This Spirit is the aid of everybody, offering to all who will accept his power a released, transformed life. The Holy Spirit is the agent in conversion, that great Christian climax which creates new people in the name and the power of Jesus.

In seeking to bring about conversion the Holy Spirit is the great preparer. The Holy Spirit has an interior access to the minds and hearts of men and women, an access denied to human beings. As Dr. Colin Williams says: "God interferes in the lives of men and women, seeking to start them on the road to salvation." Hence the preacher can point to dissatisfaction, disillusionment with life as it is, and say that this is the Holy Spirit at work disturbing, leading on to the fullness of life God plans for every person.

Conversion is the work of the Holy Spirit. No preacher, no evangelist ever converted anybody. Yet we are not helpless, for the Spirit works in us. There is a revealing sentence in the epistle to the Corinthians. Paul says, "No man can say Jesus is Lord except by the Holy Spirit" (1 Cor. 12:3). Negatively this declares how limited and helpless we all are. Positively it is making a great promise. It is declaring that the moment comes when, in the consciousness of men and women, the Spirit brings about his own revelation. This miracle happens when the personal discovery comes and the truth dawns. Jesus is Lord.

Every Sunday night in Sydney's church in-a-theater, the Lyceum Theatre, an open appeal is given for men and women to make a commitment to Jesus Christ. As that final, tense moment of appeal arrives I can look around that theater and see people who in previous months or years had been brought by the Spirit of God to conversion. Sunday by Sunday a small group of people responds. Some are disappointing and do not continue in the new life they have sought to grasp. There are others who stand firm, to whom the moment of commitment was a creative turning point in their experience. They go on to grow as Christians and to take their place in the serving and witnessing life of the church.

I think of one man, sitting with his wife, who caught my eye as the appeal proceeded on a recent Sunday night. I recall his story. One wet, cold winter's night this man was walking in loneliness the streets of Sydney. Finding a theater open he entered, expecting entertainment. Discovering it to be an act of worship, he stayed in the foyer listening through the amplification system to the message. When the appeal was given he entered, walked up the aisle of the theater, and made his commitment to Jesus Christ. Later I learned his story. Born out of wedlock, he had grown up in a children's institution. At fourteen he had run away and joined a circus. He had remained touring Australia with that circus until that night in Sydney when he was twenty-five years of age. In his life there had been no contact with the Christian church, yet for sometime a restlessness and frustration had come over him. That night in commitment something very real happened in his life. He entered the fellowship of the church and began to grow as a follower of Jesus. Presently he met and married one of the fine young people of the church. Now years later with his small family, he continues in fellowship and in service. He tells humbly and gratefully of that June night when, through conversion, God opened for him a totally new life.

In proclaiming the message of the Holy Spirit we can point to his ministry on the other side of conversion. Conversion is, of course, not an ending, but the beginning of a new endless highway which beckons on into the future.

In a perplexed and uncertain age, the Holy Spirit can be offered as the giver of what John Wesley never tired of calling assurance. He based his convictions on the words of St. Paul: "When we cry, Abba Father, it is the Spirit himself bearing witness with our spirit that we are the children of God" (Rom. 8:15-16). This witness is of sins forgiven, of acceptance, reconciliation with God. So tremendous a happening cannot take place without our knowing it. As John Wesley says: "I saw well, no one could in the nature of things, have such a sense of forgiveness and not feel it."

Assurance is not reassurance. It is far more than merely becoming aware of the providence or the benign care of God. Assurance lies on the other side of repentance and faith and of the upheaval which goes with conversion. It is the inner sense of God's presence which declares all alienation is over and a new intimate relationship with God has been established.

The Holy Spirit, from this point on, operates as the means of Christian growth. As Jesus promised, the Spirit is available as guide, counselor, strengthener. "The spirit helps us in our weakness" (Rom. 8:26).

The blessings of the Holy Spirit in the life of the Christian are without end. This we can declare. Once the Spirit of God floods into the human soul, healing and wholeness are carried to every level of personality. There come a release, a joy, which elevate life into a new dimension.

Without formalizing the so-called gifts and fruits of the Spirit, the power which the Holy Spirit brings to the life of all who trust him cannot be exaggerated. Paul tells us all about it in his comprehensive Galatian summary: "The fruit of the Spirit is love, joy, peace, patience, kindness, goodness, faithfulness, gentleness, self-control" (Gal. 5:22-23).

We miss the range and depth of the meaning of the Holy Spirit if we speak of him only in personal terms. The Holy Spirit, as Jesus clearly declared, is at work in the world. Jesus said when the Holy Spirit comes: "He will convince the world concerning sin and righteousness and judgment" (John 16:8).

This is just what the Holy Spirit has been doing in our time. All over the world there has been a discovery of the pain of unemployment, of poverty, and of racial prejudice. War has exploded in the consciousness of humanity as a vast ethical problem. Mankind everywhere has a sense of standing under judgment. A vision of a higher righteousness in human relationships has come. So the world in this second half of the twentieth century is in uproar, as the struggle for a freer and juster world goes on.

Why has it happened? I believe it is the work of the Holy Spirit. All over the world, in differing countries and differing cultures, the same ferment is at work, like yeast in a lump of dough. It is the work of the Holy Spirit. God is active in his world, calling people everywhere to see his larger plans for all people. The social, world dimensions of the operation of the Holy Spirit must be presented. It is a vital part of the message of evangelism today.

The Kingdom of God

The message for mission must today include the challenge of the kingdom of God. It is the neglect of the kingdom of God which has in part led to the distortion of an exclusively personal evangelism. The concept of the kingdom of God can redress the balance and give again to evangelism a truly full or total gospel.

The kingdom of God was a master-passion of Jesus. From the beginning to the end of his ministry he preached about the kingdom. At the commencement of his ministry he entered Galilee saying: "Repent, for the kingdom of heaven is at hand" (Matt. 3:2). Again and again he commenced his parables by saying: The kingdom is like . . . In his teachings he sought constantly to expound the meaning of the Kingdom of God on earth. In his journey to Jerusalem he sharpened his teaching and his challenge concerning his coming kingdom. During almost the last moment of his life as he hung on the cross it was of the kingdom he spoke. He responded to the plea of the dying thief beside him: "Remember me when you come into your kingdom" (Luke 23:42). In other words, at the very center of the mind of Jesus was the concept of the kingdom of God.

In view of how much the kingdom of God meant to Jesus it is strange that it has been so seriously neglected in Christian history. It is almost entirely absent from the mind and writing of St. Paul. The historic creeds of the church make no mention of it. In the Apostle's Creed, the declaration of faith jumps from "born of the virgin Mary" to "suffered under Pontius Pilate." The kingdom of God does not rate a mention.

Throughout Christian history probably fewer sermons have been preached on the kingdom of God than on any other aspect of the teachings of Jesus. In America the Methodist Church does have its "kingdom-tide" emphasis, but it is almost unique in today's church for such a place to be given to the concept of the Kingdom of God.

What explains this strange neglect? It is difficult to answer this question. Here in the mind of Jesus is a magnificent vision, the vision of society under the authority of God. Beside the vision of the kingdom of God today's kingdoms of socialism or capitalism or communism are pale by comparison. Yet somehow Christians have rarely thrilled to the glory of the kingdom of God.

What is the meaning of the phrase kingdom of God? Dr. James Moffatt described the kingdom as "the reign of God in human society." Dr. Shafto calls it "a kingdom of right relationships." With this kind of meaning, a spelling out of the kingdom of God and its significance for today provides the basis for the social witness of evangelism.

We stand today in the presence of the first world revolution. The three great issues—namely poverty, race, and war—are coalescing to create the greatest upheaval of all time. It is not in one nation or on one continent that ferment and change have developed, it is in all the earth. Evangelism must be heard, in quickened conscience, striving for deliverance from poverty, racism, and war.

Relating the message of the kingdom of God to poverty must begin with stirring the conscience of humanity concerning the depth of the crisis now facing all mankind. Somehow millions of people are shutting their eyes to the desperate misery of millions. The population explosion plus the limited organization and distribution of the resources of the earth make famine a possible catastrophe of a scale never known in history. Yet blithely millions of people go on their way, ignorant and unconcerned about the mountain of human suffering all around them.

The blunt fact is that unless a food production explosion matches the population explosion, nothing but tragedy lies ahead for hundreds of millions of human beings. Dr. Revelle, director of the Harvard Center for Population Studies, believes that food production must increase threefold by the end of the century to keep up with world demands. Already food shortages are apparent, even in the affluent West, and the fast escalation of food prices is the first sign of coming shortages and famine. How can evangelism close its eyes to this threat to human well-being, to this element of our brother's and sister's needs? To declare the kingdom of God in terms of economic justice is one of the greatest needs of our times.

The world's race issue moves into a new dimension. Unlike the poverty issue, the question of race has gripped the minds of both Christians and non-Christians alike. In one sense the racial battle has been won. Nobody defends racial prejudice any more. On the broad front of forcing an awareness of the problems of race and the acceptance of racial equality and justice and right, the struggle is over. There are, of course, pockets of areas such as in South Africa where this is not true, but broadly speaking the race issue is settled, and settled in the right way.

Now, however, the race issue moves from being an ideological struggle to the task of expressing practically what racial justice means in economic terms, in housing, in education, and spiritual opportunity.

In Australia, with its relatively minor racial problem, the immediate task is becoming apparent. Now must come the slow, painstaking analysis of particular problems and the opening of the doors one by one to Aboriginal people so they can find a life that is worthy of them. This means in Australia the grappling with problems of land rights, housing, education, and hygiene and relating the Christian gospel to the primitive faith of the people. In very practical terms the principle enunciated by the New Testament must be expressed: "There is neither Jew nor Greek, there is neither slave nor free, there is neither male nor female; for you are all one in Christ" (Gal. 3:28).

The message of the kingdom of God, in international terms, must, I believe, be the proclamation of a message of nonviolence.

War has now become impossible. In a nuclear age, mankind cannot make war and live. Slowly this conviction is dawning on human consciousness. Hence again and again there has been a drawing back from the precipice of an atomic catastrophe.

What then is the message for mission today? I claim it must be a call to nonviolence. Jesus was the greatest nonviolent leader in history. The Sermon on the Mount is perhaps the worlds finest document of nonviolence. The whole teaching and example of Jesus declare his central utterance: "Put your sword back into its place; for all who take the sword will perish by the sword" (Matt. 26:52).

The threat of violence now moves from the international to the national scene. There are those who claim that justice can only be advanced by a resort to violence —hence the support for guerilla activity even among some Christians. My view is that it would be a tragedy if, just at a time when we are turning away from the "just war" concept, we should find attractive the idea of a "just revolution." There must be change, and drastic change around the world, but the means of change in my view cannot be, and must not be, violence.

In this kind of world the Christian message of nonviolence becomes crucial. Here in this teaching of Jesus is a means of social change that does not inject into history further hatred and bitterness. Here is action which can both transform and redeem at one and the same time. I am convinced that at this hour the Christian preacher and evangelist have a tremendously relevant word to say—it is to point to the nonviolence of Jesus. We stand today at the point foreseen by Martin Luther King when he said: "The choice is no longer between violence and nonviolence. It is either nonviolence or nonexistence."

THE METHOD OF MISSION

If ever Marshall McLuhan's claim that "the medium is the message" were true, it is true of the Christian church. The Christian gospel and the Christian church are inextricably bound up together. The church is part of the fact of Jesus Christ. For good or ill, as humanity sees it, the church is the message.

Let me say at once, I believe in the church. I do not see it today as moribund or destined for oblivion. The church, in spite of its many failures, is making a better effort to adjust to rapid social change than most of the established institutions of society. It is updating its thinking and practices far more effectively than, shall we say, the institution of the presidency in America, or the monarchy in Britain, or trade unions, or many of the agencies of education.

Look at what has happened over the last quarter of a century. There can be listed many achievements in the life of the church. First the World Council of Churches was born in 1948 at Amsterdam. That first assembly of the World Council of Churches was an event of historic proportions. The second Vatican Council under the inspired leadership of Pope John came to pass. It has released unpredictable influences for change through the vast and ancient structure of the Roman Catholic Church. The charismatic revival has moved across the world bringing, in spite of its excesses in some places, renewal and release to Christian people and Christian communities.

The Jesus Revolution has emerged among young people all over the world, and while now it seems to be running its course, it has projected the personality of Jesus into the youth culture of our time in an almost miraculous way.

There is today a proliferation of experimental ministries within the Christian church. Undoubtedly more new forms of Christian witness and activity are being attempted than perhaps for centuries in the life of the church. It may be that soon more general principles will emerge from this experimentation which will guide the church as a whole forward.

During the last fifteen years many Christians and some parts of the corporate life of the churches have taken a worthy part in the protest movement against poverty, racism, and war. Christians have often plunged into the struggle for justice and freedom—as evidenced by the imprisonment of Christian leaders in South Korea and the Philippines, in the witness of Archbishop Camara of northeastern Brazil, and the men and women who led the struggles against racial discrimination and the Vietnam war in America, in the courage of the World Council of Churches' leadership against apartheid in South Africa. I believe the church can afford to be judged by the place Christians have taken in the liberation movements of recent years.

I have confidence in the role of the local Christian community, the sometimes despised suburban and rural church. Far from being outmoded, the local churches in suburban rural and city areas are today more relevant than ever. In the kind of mass society being fashioned under our eyes, trends are moving toward the local church, not away from it. Amid the impersonal, lonely mass society, the creation of local groups of Christians is utterly essential if millions of people are to find a sense of belonging, if they are to find personal identity, dignity, and worth.

However there is much, so very much, to be done if the Christian church is to fulfill its promise and match the opportunities which will arise in the remaining years of the twentieth century. To begin speaking about the method of mission, it is essential to speak mainly about the church. The world mission of Jesus must be carried on primarily through local Christian communities across the world. It is within these small societies of Jesus that the new evangelism must express itself. The basic unit for mission is the neighborhood church; there the new life of God must appear.

The Centrality of Worship

The Christian church possesses no greater instrument for mission than worship. Millions of Christians gather Sunday by Sunday around the world to worship God. No assembly of people has proved so persistent and powerful as the weekly worshiping community. The natural center for mission is the worshipping community,

66

inspired and informed, moving out from worship to witness in the world.

There is something that has gone drastically wrong in modern worship. It arises from the fact that worship has become almost exclusively nurture, its evangelical purpose being lost. Worship must include the nurture of Christians, but it must also be the proclamation of the gospel of Jesus to those who have not yet received it.

In the Methodist Church in Great Britain it used to be said that the minister preached to the saints in the morning and to the sinners at night. Unfortunately, with the coming of television night worship in many places has declined or disappeared. The result is that the poor, old "sinners" are missing out. The missionary purpose of worship has passed into eclipse.

I confess to being greatly influenced by a discovery I made from church history years ago. In the early church there were two forms of worship. One form represented the gathering of Christians for nurture and strengthening through the breaking of bread from house to house. However, there was a second form of worship that was designed primarily for pagans. It made no assumptions as to the belief of those who came and was always designed to communicate the gospel to those who did not understand it and had not accepted it.

The modern church needs to recover the insight of the early Christians. Around every church in every land is a mission field. There is a tremendous need for worship to be designed in part for those who as yet have not found a Christian commitment. Therefore one of the great and urgent needs of the church is to recover evangelical worship.

Worship designed for mission will be different. It will show characteristics which will vary greatly from worship as nurture. For many churches it will force a whole reassessment as to the time, the place, the style, the purpose of worship.

Worship seen as the church in mission would seek above all else to start where people are. This would mean assuming that people know very little about the Christian gospel. There would be a sensitivity toward such a position. Ritual, congregational responses which are based on belief, would become almost unuseable. Worship would not force prayer upon people who could not accept the basic assumptions of prayer early in a service. There would be a much slower movement into declarations of faith than in the average worship experience designed for nurture. The typical language of worship which assumes full faith would be scrutinized carefully and used sparingly. The cardinal principal would be to start where people are in the hope and expectation that there may be some who will move forward toward a fuller faith. The pace, the mood, the vitality of many acts of worship would have to be reexamined. Worship is all too often slow and sad and somber. Often, a sense of vitality and urgency is conspicuous by its absence.

In the New Testament there was a release, a joy, an excitement about worship which puzzled those who observed it. Seeing the abandon and exhilaration of the early Christians, it was thought they must be either mad or drunk. Who could imagine anyone observing a typical Sunday morning act of worship in modern local churches describing those within as either drunk or mad? There is so much decorum, so much that expresses restraint and order making for propriety and dullness.

How to draw people into the mood and emotion of worship is a major task. Somehow an intermingling of emotion, a participation in what is happening must be achieved. Much worship is too austere and intellectualized. A folksiness, a friendship must be communicated if worship is to live in power.

Music in worship is of tremendous importance. In recent years there has been a revolution in music. Lilt and joy and rhythm have been introduced into secular music, and these qualities have made it so much a part of today's culture, particularly the culture of youth. Yet in Christian worship the steady four-beat march of stately music goes on. Many churches act as though nothing has changed for a hundred years in the field of music. For example, the Presbyterian Hymn Book in Australia has no hymn in it which was written by anyone born in this century.

"Modern young people do not hear the diapason stop of an organ," a brilliant Australian organist said recently. Yet so many churches continue to put all faith in the pipe organ. Sometimes it appears as though Christians believe that the only pipe through which the Holy Spirit can blow is an organ pipe. The introduction of modern instruments and fast rhythm music are essential if in today's world music is to be a highway for the gospel.

I would like to see Sunday night redeemed for evangelical worship in many places and countries. Morning family worship, therefore, could be planned for the nurture of Christians, for the gathered community of believers. Sunday night could express the second purpose of worship, namely to reach out to those who do not as yet accept Christ. Such a development would bring back some balance into the total life and witness of the church.

I suppose I am conditioned by the experiences of my own ministry in Sydney, Australia. The church I serve, the Central Methodist Mission, owns a theater in the heart of the downtown Sydney theater district. Since 1906 the gospel has been preached in this Lyceum Theater, which during the week is a movie house but on Sunday becomes a church-in-a-theater. I confess I would rather preach in this theater in Sydney than anywhere on earth. It allows flexibility in worship, it draws people into it that would hesitate to enter an ecclesiastical building, it forces the preacher to design worship and to preach from the point where the people may be in their experience.

It is significant that in this church-in-a-theater there has assembled for almost all the years of this century the largest Sunday-night Christian congregation in Australia. This fact is not unrelated to the style of building and the nature of the worship offered within it. Sunday night at seven o'clock at the Lyceum Theater is designed as worship for mission.

THE POWER OF PREACHING

Preaching is utterly central to the mission of Jesus and the task of the church. The greatest single method for spreading the gospel is preaching. When preaching is strong and confident, the church is strong and effective. When preaching is weak and uncertain, the church is muted in its witness.

The New Testament says that Jesus came into Galilee preaching. Preaching obviously was the chosen method of Jesus. Throughout his life he gave himself to communicating the gospel by proclamation. At the end he gave his great commission to go into the world and preach the gospel.

In the long story of the Christian church the great moments of witness have been through preaching. Who can question the Christian significance of Jesus, Peter, Paul, Savanarola, Martin Luther, John Wesley, George Whitefield, William Temple, Martin Luther King? All had tremendous power in proclaiming the gospel, in the preaching of the word.

A serious fallacy has spread far through the church today; it is the so-called "presence concept." While valuable as a protest against too great a trust in merely verbalizing the gospel, the presence concept is a dangerous half truth. The presence idea is the reappearance of one of the worst features of the liberal era of theology. It claims that it is only necessary to be kind and good, to be concerned. The presence idea is filled with pharisaism, a pharisaism which claims that quality of life can be so transparent that Christ shines through. It is a denial of the evangelical faith which believes that a man must, through repentance and faith, be brought to a saving knowledge of Jesus Christ.

So the argument runs, open a coffee shop and show youth you are "with it." Serve endless cups of coffee with a smile but make no mention of Jesus Christ. Run a togetherness event to defeat the loneliness of society, but plan no moment of proclamation, therefore insuring that the event will reflect the culture and the values of

71

the society around it. Begin a counseling center, aid people to become adjusted to themselves, their neighbors, their environment, but say nothing about the fundamental need of all—adjustment and reconciliation to God. Start a community aid service or open an old folks home, but be content if creature comforts are met.

The inadequacy of the presence idea is beginning to appear. There are Christian centers, such as the East Harlem Protestant Parish, where millions of dollars have been spent and deep devotion has been given, but no adequate community of Christians has emerged from the presence approach. No one who trusts this method seems to be able to answer the question of from where will the Christian presence come in the next generation if there is a failure to fashion a Christian community, the church, now. Presence without proclamation is a failure.

I plead, therefore, for a recovery of faith in preaching. Especially is there need for evangelical preaching. To struggle for message, to give great attention not only to what is to be said but how to say it is the need. The discovery of ways of effectiveness in preaching for a verdict must be sought.

Some years ago the British preacher Dr. Russell Maltby gave six precepts for what may be termed evangelical preaching.

1. Listen before you speak. See before you say.
2. In preaching, no demand without the gift; no diagnosis without the cure.
3. One word about sin, ten for the Savior.
4. There is always water if you bore deep enough.
5. The well is deep, and you must have something to draw

with. But there is no need to make people drink out of the bucket, still less to chew the rope.
6. Love simple speech as you hate shallow thinking.

Evangelical preaching means seeking to win men and women to a commitment to Jesus Christ. Too often preachers are content to try to influence people. The task in evangelism is surely to bring people by the power of the Holy Spirit to a verdict. Each man must work out his own way of bringing the faith of people to focus. However it is done, the winning of hearers to commitment is essential for the task of mission. After all, Jesus did tell Peter to follow him, and Peter openly responded in obedience; he set out on the road with Jesus.

Preaching for conversion is an inevitable corollary to moving into an era of world mission. In places like England, America, and Australia, it has been very easy to fall into the trap of thinking everyone is a Christian—at least of a sort. The so-called mission fields were far away. Within the home countries it was natural to assume that all speaking and preaching was to a largely convinced society. Hence preaching ceased to be evangelical, and the informing, the teaching of Christians and those who came from Christian homes became the dominant purpose.

Now all is changed. Every place is a mission field. Conversion therefore becomes necessary for people who are literally coming as did the early Christians from a non-Christian position to the point of faith. Preaching for a verdict so that the conversion experience may follow is the task of all who witness for Christ's sake.

There is a directness about evangelical preaching which

needs recovering by the pulpit. To preach about the gospel is very different from preaching the gospel. Too often preachers assume too much and begin too far ahead of where the minds of their hearers really are.

There is of course a greater costliness in preaching for a goal than preaching without focus. To bring people to commitment means being at the point of commitment. It is much easier to stop short of calling for a verdict.

Yet when the price is paid in prayer and preparation, when the sacrifice is made of trying to come into focus, there is no satisfaction on earth to equal seeing someone step into the kingdom of God.

The day of preaching is not done. Preaching, proclaiming, placarding before men and women the mighty acts of God are as essential today as ever. Jesus came into Galilee preaching.

What a privilege it is to proclaim the good news of Jesus. This was forced into my consciousness with great power on a recent Easter Sunday morning. Each year in Sydney we have a sunrise service in one of the drive-in theaters of the city. Before the huge white screen a scaffolding and a platform are built. There to the people in hundreds of cars and to a television audience across Australia, we present the resurrection story each year.

Last Easter the service began with a fanfare of trumpets and proceeded with power and with joy. My own spirit, as I came to the end of the preaching of the message, was elevated, exhilarated. The Benediction was pronounced, and there came over my mind and heart a shadow. For some reason I found myself thinking that I now had one less Easter to preach the gospel. I confess that this phrase greets me as each Sunday comes. As the day ends, the thought is also there. Now you have one less Sunday to preach about Jesus. What a privilege it is to tell the greatest news that has ever fallen on human ears.

The Way of Fellowship

Christian fellowship from the beginning has been the mark of the true church of Jesus Christ. Following the birth of the church at Pentecost, two characteristics at once emerged. First there was a rich unity expressed in the practices of fellowship: they broke bread from house to house. Second they had all things in common. There appeared a primitive communism of the early church in which the church became a sacrificial, caring fellowship. As a result, people looking on this new phenomenon said, not in cynicism but in wonder, "See how these Christians love one another."

The offering of fellowship in a mass society is part of the contribution the Christian faith has to offer in today's world. To create fellowship is part of the strategy of mission. With worship must go the creation of fellowship.

Loneliness is a deep, modern sickness of soul. It is far more serious in the lives of people than we recognize. There is an old Latin proverb which declares: "One man is half a man." The French writer Sartre said: "Without a looker-on, a man evaporates." The Bible, of course, from the beginning makes this same emphasis: It is not good for man to be alone. In other words, men and women are made for fellowship. When it is there joy can be full,

75

when it is absent suffering is acute. In the many hundreds of suicide situations that have been faced in the Life Line Centre in Sydney, loneliness is in a majority of cases a major cause of despair. All manner of human predicaments are compounded by loneliness.

Society today is multiplying lonely people by the millions. So many characteristics of modern society increase the isolation and alienation of people. God's plan was obviously that people should find strength in the family. Today millions of families are being crushed by the pressures of mass society. The smaller units of society are disappearing, engulfed by larger institutions which alone seem able to survive. Machines and computers depersonalize people. Among the poor even the friendliness of the slums is being replaced by the isolation of apartment houses.

All this is creating the terrifying big society where the individual scarcely seems to count. I think of an incident in our own family circle. The postman one day brought the eagerly awaited news whether one of our sons would be admitted into the Australian university of his choice. Our son opened the letter, and his face fell, for he had missed gaining a place in the university quota. However, the fact which seemed to eat into his spirit most was that the letter stated his place had been determined by a computer. He said with some bitterness: "To think my career, my life, is being determined by a blessed machine."

In confronting this kind of lonely impersonal society, the Christian church has the opportunity of offering fellowship at two levels. It can create the fellowship of the parachurch and seek to serve the community by offering places and activities of interest to all people. Through such centers and organizations interpersonal relationships can be fashioned.

Secondly, the church can offer to those who have a common faith in Jesus Christ a deeper richness of fellowship. Fellowship then has as its basic purpose nurture and growth for all who are committed to Jesus Christ.

I have become convinced of the value, as an evangelical method, of the parachurch. By parachurch I mean a halfway church, not half a church. The simple fact is that masses of people now in many societies are so far removed from the Christian church that it is unlikely that they will suddenly enter into its buildings or become part of its worship or its fellowship. There must be some way by which stepping stones or a bridge may be built over which people living beyond the church may move to accept its fellowship. By creating parachurch activities such a way can develop.

It is scandalous that all over the Western world there stand piles of masonry in the form of Christian churches and centers often in centrally located sites which are closed and deserted for most of the week. Often these huge church properties stand amid teeming community need, yet they remain barred and locked against the people who could be served by the churches. A heavy judgment will fall on the church if it cannot find a way of creatively placing back into circulation the resources in buildings and leadership it possesses. By the development of a seven-day-a-week program and the modification of existing properties, the Sunday isolation of the church can be broken down.

In 1964 the church center where I serve in Sydney

was gutted by fire. We at once faced the challenge of building for at least the remaining years of the century. We called on one of Australia's research organizations to assist. We asked what, in their view, would be the nature of society leading up to the year 2000. The report and conclusions which they gave us were simple yet profound. The coming society, said that report, will reveal three features: increasing affluence, increasing leisure, and increasing loneliness.

Out of the ashes of the fire and armed with the insights of this report, we built Wesley Centre in the heart of downtown Sydney. It is a building wrapped around an idea, the idea of combating loneliness in a big city, of offering fellowship through parachurch activities to the people. In this building there are four floors given to community activities. Seven days a week there is an attempt made to meet the community needs of the people.

Unorganized fellowship is offered. Many churches fall into the trap of only welcoming people and serving them by trying to organize them. Whenever anybody steps into a church property it is for a particular organizational involvement. Yet many do not wish always to be regimented. The very nature of our complex and highly organized society makes people want to be free in leisure time.

In Wesley Centre we have developed what is called the Wesley Club. It turns the building into a drop-in center for old and young. In pleasant lounges with eating and other facilities, people are able to make it a meeting place, a friendship center. We have been surprised at the number of people who have been ready to pay a small fee of four dollars a year in order to have membership in a Christian club in the heart of the city. Far more significant are the organizational groups, some built on interest, some built on the basis of age. Literally hundreds of people find satisfaction and fellowship together in the programs of a parachurch.

Let me give two illustrations. We have established a singles society. On learning that in the city of Sydney, a metropolis of three million people, there are 569,000 people living as singles, we felt something special should be done for them. Drawing together a small group of people the idea of a new society was projected. After planning, after several months of experimental programing we felt ready to announce to the city that a singles society was in being.

The Singles Society meets on a Friday night. It begins with a dinner at which a visiting speaker discusses current affairs. There follows an assembly with a period of Christian devotions. At eight o'clock there are ten activities available, from dancing and games for those who only want to relax for the evening, to drama, art, and Bible study groups, and to personal-growth groups for people with more serious interests. Throughout the evening a coffee shop operates and is particularly popular once the groups conclude. Rich fellowship is found through midnight, as background music is played and folk singers entertain. Beyond the Friday night are many activities, such as harbor cruises, dances, excursions, barbeques, weekend conferences.

We have been amazed at the response to the Singles Society. Hundreds of people have come, and it has been fascinating to watch a new community of people develop. Many who have lived in isolation have been drawn together, and lives are becoming intertwined in interest and activity. Many are coming into the life of the church, thus moving towards the richest fellowship of all, that which is found in worship and the sacraments.

During two days of the week another age group meets. It is the largest of the parachurch activities, the School for Seniors. Through medical science people live longer today, and yet still many retire at sixty or sixty-five years of age. Many therefore face perhaps twenty years of retirement. These can be purposeless, empty years. Life is too valuable for so long a period to be spent in trifling pastimes in an effort to kill time. The School for Seniors has been operating for years. We are able to offer some twenty-eight classes for people who can make their choices, moving from group to group on an hourly basis throughout the day. The dominant feature of this school is the quality of fellowship that develops. It has also revealed unsuspected abilities and skills in people who now have the opportunity to take up latent interests. Again it has been exciting to see the contribution fellowship makes to people in this lonely world. We have even made the interesting discovery that some people have put up their age saying they are older than they really are in order to qualify at the age of fifty-five, which is the age for entering the School for Seniors. There has been a striking response to the tune of fifteen hundred members to the school's call to keep growing all your life.

There is a deeper fellowship which must be offered by a church in mission. The fellowship of the parachurch is open to people who have not yet arrived at any com-

80

mitment to Jesus Christ. The deeper fellowship of the church can really only be discovered by those who have come to know God in Jesus Christ. It is a fellowship found in Christian unity and spiritual growth. Hence fellowship as nurture must be part of the strategy of the church.

One of the great weaknesses of evangelism has always been what follows after the moment of commitment to Jesus Christ. Unless the church provides opportunities for new Christians to meet and to grow, it lacks an essential element in its ministry. In one sense there is no such thing as a Christian, for all of us are always only becoming Christians. Any adequate evangelism must provide facilities for personal growth, both in spiritual experience and the intellectual understanding of the Christian's faith.

No church is complete which does not have its adult Christian education program. Ways by which people can come to know in greater depth the Bible and Christian doctrines are essential. Every living, growing Christian community must enroll its people in a school for Christians.

Yet intellectual growth is not enough. The deep nurture of the spirit is essential. However it is done, spiritual-growth groups must be part of the whole program of any vital church. Through Bible study, through testimony and sharing, through prayer, through caring for each other, lives are drawn together and people are aided to discover further the mystery and the wonder of God and his purposes for the world.

In our program in Sydney, the offering of fellowship through the parachurch and as nurture come together in the camping and conference life of our people. On the outskirts of Sydney, just twenty-six miles from the heart of the city, we have recently obtained seventy acres in a beautiful hidden valley amid the Australian gum trees. There, what is called Vision Valley has developed.

Vision Valley has been described as a Christian country center for everyone. To this center all groups of the church go for weekends and vacation periods, where a greater depth of fellowship can be developed through people living together for a longer period than the time it takes to hold a meeting in a church.

At Vision Valley there are lodges where 150 people can stay in motel comfort. There are all the facilities required for eating and entertainment, teaching and worship. There are horses for riding and canoes on a small manmade lake, a swimming pool, and hiking trails through the bush. There is provision for worship in a small historic chapel which is actually the oldest Methodist chapel in Australia, reerected in the valley. There is also an open-air place for worship, called the Gum Tree Chapel. In the quietness of the Australian countryside and the beauty of the bush, people are encouraged to find fellowship with depth in the context of the Christian interpretation of life.

The followers of Jesus have a tremendous asset in the fellowship his spirit creates. The church, as the world's most open society, is equipped as no other institution on earth to offer acceptance and caring to all people. To develop the fellowship potential of the Christian church is part of the task of mission. Through fellowship the kingdom of God expands.

The Serving Church

The church which only worships dies. Worship is utterly central to the ministry of Jesus in the world, as we have said, but unless worship flows out in service and witness, it loses its power. Therefore, finding ways of serving the needs of the people is the essence of the gospel.

The call to serve as part of mission arises directly from the teaching and example of Jesus. How sensitive was the compassionate heart of Jesus Christ. His soul responded to every form of human need. He could not bypass pain. The New Testament tells us that over and over again he had compassion for the multitude. He seemed unable to reject any cry for help from somebody in need. Jesus did not wait to be asked for help. He broke the Jewish Sabbath and scandalized the Pharisees, building up a hatred which was to end in His death. He did this rather than refuse to help people in distress. His spirit just could not endure to see unanswered misery. Love broke through every barrier.

We are able to peer into the compassionate mind of Jesus, not only through what he did but through what he said. In the two greatest parables he ever told, the key word is compassion. The father of the prodigal son had compassion on him and ran to greet him, forgiving him. The good Samaritan had compassion for the injured man lying helpless on the Jericho road. The compassion of Jesus finds its greatest expression in words in the prayer spoken on the cross, directed toward his enemies; "Father, forgive them; for they know not what they do" (Luke 23:34).

83

If we are to find God in power for mission we must be in service for him.

The Australian poet, Ken Walsh, writes:

O God,
Where are you?
Here.
Where?
Here in this person
And this person and this person.
But Lord,
I loathe some of these people.
I know,
But this is where
You'll find me.

Several years ago in Australia, the Methodist Conference of New South Wales carried a resolution stating: "All worshipping congregations are urged to find a service project through which corporately they can express Christian concern." This resolution has led to much social activity throughout the state. Churches have, as congregational projects, opened day nurseries in new housing areas, built homes for the aged, undertaken community aid services, started life-line telephone counseling ministries. This development has been one of the most significant in recent years in Australia because it has given to the people a vision of an incarnate Christ who is involved in the suffering and the needs of the people.

With the sociological methods available today, it is possible to analyze a community and reliably discover where people are in need and what problems they are facing. By this kind of analysis the church can gain its insight as to what it may do to fulfill its servant purpose. Inspired by the example of a serving church, people are more ready to listen to the message of the Christian.

There are some who argue that the church should contract out of the scene of social service, of meeting the needs of people in the community. Cannot government departments and secular agencies look after the needy? I would claim that the church must stay in this field of meeting human need. It must continue to be the servant church for the sake of the people and for the sake of its own soul. If Christians are maneuvered to where they can only talk about the gospel rather than to reveal in deeds the mercy of Christ, distortion overtakes the whole area of witness. The church needs to remain in this field for the people's sake. The Christian church can bring a motive, an atmosphere, a goal to social service which can be found nowhere else save through those who serve for Christ's sake.

In social service motive is paramount. A recent survey has shown in America that the secular hot-line-type of telephone ministry has only had a limited life-span of two years. The "do-gooder" approach to meeting human need can be very temporary and inadequate. In Christian social service there can be a divine plus sign which makes the difference. If an aged persons' home has around it the horizons of eternity, it can have a very different atmosphere compared with the secular institution, where the great Christian hope of eternal life is unheard. As life lengthens attitudes are very different if people believe they have one foot in heaven rather than one foot in the grave.

Similarly in the area of counseling, there is an additional dimension when it is carried on in the context of Christian belief. Secular counseling undoubtedly can aid people to become adjusted to themselves, to others, and to their environment. However, there is another basic adjustment which is necessary for wholeness of life, namely adjustment to God. It is the Christian counseling service which adds this new dimension to the caring and counseling of people.

The Christian telephone counseling ministry which is now spreading to many cities around the world is an example of the outreach in service of the Christian church. The first center was opened in Sydney, Australia, in 1963. By the use of trained Christian lay persons it was able to say to the people that help is as close as the telephone. From this first center offering a round-the-clock service to the people, an idea has spread. As I write there are well above one hundred cities linked in this international ministry of compassion. Literally thousands of lay people are expressing their Christian faith in this form of service. There are now over one million telephone calls each year coming to these centers in different countries. The life-line telephone ministry is setting out to establish a network of compassion around the world. (It is known "Contact" in the United States.)

So much in today's society requires operation on an international basis. In commerce and industry, in education and in science, in entertainment and in sport, all is developing more and more on an international basis. Similarly, there is a need for an international caring concern. Human need does not stop at national boundaries or at the coastline of continents.

The need for an international caring agency was shown

in an incident which developed from the Sydney life-line telephone center. One day the telephone call was from a distraught father who had just received a telephone call from his daughter in Washington, D.C. She had called to say good-bye, for she was planning to commit suicide. The father turned to the Sydney center asking for help. Within ten minutes the telephone lines were cleared across the Pacific, and the Sydney center was talking to a Christian minister in Washington. Within another half an hour he was at the girl's apartment and was able to draw her back from the edge of that precipice of suicide. Care and consideration were given to her by the church while she remained in Washington. Three months later a grateful family came to the Sydney center, and the girl said simply, "I did not know so many people cared."

The purpose of the serving ministry is to meet human need. It is not carried on in order to make people Christian, to maneuver them toward conversion. However, the fact remains that a caring ministry does predispose men and women to hear the gospel. When Christians show no concern toward human suffering people are less ready to listen to the spoken message which may be uttered.

The goal of service is to meet people's needs in body, mind, and spirit. The Christian church must be concerned to meet the needs of the whole man and the whole woman and not to forget the world of the Spirit. Evangelism and social service do belong together.

Preparing the Highway

In an age when masses of people live perpetually beyond the regular ministries of the church, a way to reach them must be found. Somehow, with a modern twist of meaning, the cry of John the Baptist must be heard: "Prepare the way of the Lord, make his paths straight" (Matt. 3:3). John Wesley, in his day, found the way through field preaching. Breaking with tradition, he went out to the people, gathering great crowds in the open air to hear the gospel. One of the secrets of the evangelical revival in England in the eighteenth century was that John Wesley and his followers found a way of reaching the people.

The modern approach is obviously through mass media. A highway exists for speaking to and influencing people such as history has never seen. Radio, films, television, the printed page reach and affect the lives of almost all the people all the time. Few if any of the changes of the twentieth century equal the impact of the multimedia revolution. The new evangelism of the church must set out to use the vast communication highways of today for the gospel's sake. There simply is no way of reaching people in a mass society except by using means of mass communication.

There are four basic principles which must be accepted in proclaiming the Christian message through mass media. First, any Christian message on such media as radio and television must be directed toward and fashioned for people who do not as yet accept the Christian position. To use mass media for the nurture of Christians is an exercise in futility, the wasting of an immense opportunity for evangelism. Second, there are limits to the way mass means of communication can be used beyond which the Christian church cannot go. There is a blanket, manipulative type of presentation available and used by the advertising world which must be rejected by Christians. Dr. Herbert Farmer said in his book, *The Servant of the Word* (London: Nisbet & Co., 1941). "The preacher must deeply reverence in his hearer what has been called the sacred power of rejection, even in the midst of his passionate desire for acceptance" (p. 73). That principle certainly applies to radio and television. Third, the message presented through mass media must not be about the gospel of Jesus, it must be the gospel itself. It is at this point that so much falls short in Christian programs. They assume too much, they are not direct enough; they are concerned with secondary truths or inconsequential aspects of the Christian faith instead of, to use John Wesley's notable phrase, "offering men Christ." Fourth, mass media is a contact method without comparison; but of itself it is not enough. The gospel is in its essence a person-to-person affair and must issue in the creation of fellowship, the establishment of new relationships. How to follow up any gains registered in the minds and lives of people at the receiving end of mass media must forever be the concern of the church.

There are few more interesting examples of how something, threatened with extinction, fought back and lived than the story of the survival of modern radio. When television arrived it seemed that radio was finished. On the contrary; so effectively has it accommodated itself to change, aided of course by the transistor revolution, that radio is more effective and powerful than ever.

As one who constantly uses both radio and television, I can only say that in the communication of religious truth radio is more effective than television. From periods when I have had both regular radio and television programs, evidence has shown the superior power of radio in the influencing of people's lives. Whether it is the added concentration of listening and not seeing or the intimacy of radio which is used by people individually rather than group-watching as in television, the fact remains of the effectiveness of radio.

The Christian church in most places has made alarmingly inadequate use of radio. When it is remembered that the vast millions of people in the third world cannot afford nor are likely to be able to possess television, the place of radio is assured. It is in radio that the church should be investing both its money and its specially trained people. Radio could be a vital highway of the Lord in today's world.

Television is made for preaching. By that I mean it is a natural medium for the conveying of truth from mind to mind through the power of personality. This judgment, I realize, runs counter to the conviction of many who work in the field of television. The indirect approach, the documentary, the endless panel discussions, and drama all have their places. However, nothing has proved more effective in America than the Bishop Fulton Sheen telecasts, and that was almost straight preaching. In Australia no religious television series has obtained the ratings of the seven-year-long "I Challenge the Minister" program. It was one man standing before an audience on the beach, in a factory, at a university, on the wharves and answering questions. It was simply an open-air meeting of the kind presented by Lord Soper at

Tower Hill and Hyde Park in London, with the television cameras rolling.

According to some of the world's most successful religious publishers, there is an astonishing interest in religious books. Yet how disturbing it is that in a typical secular bookshop in the west there are probably more books available on astrology and the occult than on the Christian faith.

The reason? It is because not enough Christian books are published with a broad evangelical purpose. Religious literature like so much else designed by Christians is written for Christian believers. How great is the need in evangelism for what used to be called Apologetics, for pamphleteering for the grappling with the really fundamental issues of the reality of God as Father, Son, and Holy Spirit and the offering in modern language and presentation of the way of salvation!

Any new evangelism literature must deal with the question of distribution. So much that is written lies, selling only in tens and twenties, on the shelves of religious bookshops or at book tables of churches. Beyond is the vast reading public untapped, unreached.

The World Methodist Council has produced three small books for World Mission 1975. They carry the titles: *How Can I Find God? Who Really Is Jesus?* and *What Is the Meaning of Life?* The name given to this series is "Pass It On Books." Christians are challenged to accept ten copies of each title and to give away or sell them to people who would not claim to be worshiping, practicing Christians. It is but one small experiment aimed at using the highways of mass media for the gospel today.

THE STRUGGLE FOR A JUST SOCIETY

The new evangelism must find a message and a method which will radically change the world. An evangelism which is purely individualistic in its purpose and effect is largely irrelevant in today's world and has little chance of reaching a mass of people with the good news of Jesus Christ. Only by a recovery of the prophetic element of the Old and the New Testaments can modern Christianity again become a vital force.

The greatest single burden which evangelism carries is the story of its irrelevance, even its positive harm in the past in the struggle for justice and freedom. There have been Christians in the past who have consciously or unconsciously espoused the evangelical message because it offered an alternative to drastic social change. Hence evangelism seemed to leave untouched the sorrows of the early industrial revolution, the tragedy of slavery, and the unbelievable misery of poverty.

Dr. James H. Cone in his book *A Black Theology of Liberation* (Philadelphia: J. B. Lippincott Company, 1970), expresses the resentment that many feel. "Black theology must counsel black people to beware of the Wesley brothers and their concern for personal salvation, the warm heart and all that stuff. What black people do not need are warm hearts. Our attention must be elsewhere—say the political, social and economic freedom of black people" (p. 72).

This statement is quoted not only because it shows the seething resentment of the dispossessed but because it also reveals the error in another direction to which such moods can lead. When the Christian message says

92

there is no need of the warm heart, it is really saying an experience of God in Jesus Christ is not necessary. If this became the alternate to evangelism it would be as distorted as pietism and fail to bring to people the liberation they have craved.

However, let us face it, for centuries salvation in Christian terms has contained two elements: the saving of souls by subtracting them out of the body and out of society and the saving of people not so much to live a fuller life now, but to find fulfillment beyond the grave.

Salvation today must be the receiving of God's saving grace for the whole person, body, mind, and spirit. Father Gustavo Gutierrez in A Theology of Liberation declares how the new evangelism must look. He writes: "The center of God's salvific design is Jesus Christ, who by His death and resurrection transforms the universe and makes it possible for man to reach fulfillment as a human being. This fulfillment embraces every aspect of humanity; body, and spirit, individual and society, person and cosmos, time and eternity" (p. 151).

Jesus must at one and the same time be presented as a personal savior and a cultural exorcist. The whole world cries out for a power which can give freedom to communities that are possessed by evil. Slavery, racism, anti-Semitism, or a war fever can place whole societies in bondage. For example a pro-Vietnam mentality enslaved America and Australia for years. Christ, as with the eventual overthrow of slavery, has proved his power to defeat corporate evil and set the people free from their obsessions.

Modern evangelism cannot shut its eyes to poverty. Poverty as the expression of the iniquity of the present economic order of society must be the concern of the gospel. The world is in the process of discovering poverty in its towering dimensions almost for the first time. To quote Father Gutierrez again: "It is only in the last few years that people have become aware of the scope and the misery in which the great majority of mankind exists" (p. 64).

Poverty statistics are stunning. There are seven hundred million illiterate people in the world, two hundred million more than twenty years ago. There are two hundred and thirty million people unemployed. There are three hundred and ninety million lives nearing starvation. There are one thousand, three hundred million who are undernourished.

Bishop Gore once said that "Christian love means reading statistics with compassion." Here is how poverty looks when interpreted by love.

Poverty is overcrowded living where privacy is unknown.

Poverty is illiteracy, with masses of people unable to reach full development.

Poverty is hunger, pitiable hunger with starvation an ever present peril.

Poverty is weariness because of unbalanced diets and malnutrition.

Poverty is the terrible idleness of unemployment.

Poverty is exploitation by people, of people, and through the power of impersonal forces.

Poverty is being emotionally, culturally deprived.

Poverty is spiritual deadness, for it is hard to hear the voice of God with an empty stomach.

Even in affluent Australia there are half a million hidden poor. But if measured beside the suffering of the third world, Australian poverty must seem like riches. Yet in the affluent West there are people who must not be forgotten. The Australian poet Ken Walsh has glimpsed them.

> Two migrant women—
> (Mother and daughter)
> Their faces marked
> By dark shadows
> Under their eyes.
>
> Waiting
> (With their children)
> In an old car
> Outside,
> A real estate office.

There is no doubt where God stands in this world struggle for a just society. The biblical God is a liberating God. Whenever God is presented in the Bible, he is on the side of the poor, the slaves, the outcast, the oppressed. Standing among them he works to set them free. God is a revolutionary God.

Look at the evidence. Right at the beginning of the biblical story is the release of the slaves from Egypt. The basis of the story is a message which came to Moses from God, and he said: "I have seen the affliction of my people who are in Egypt, . . . and I have come down to deliver them" (Exod. 3:7, 8). One day the great prophet Jeremiah stood at the gate of the temple and protested against the hypocrisy of a religion which was not concerned with the poor. Amend your ways, he shouted,

95

end your oppression of the stranger, the alien, the fatherless, the widow.

When Mary grappled with the meaning of the child who was to be born to her, she said, in what we call the Magnificat: "My soul magnifies the Lord, He has put down the mighty from their throne, He has filled the hungry with good things, and the rich He has sent empty away." When Jesus was born it was in a stable and to a poverty-stricken home in Palestine. Dr. James Cone said to be born in a manger would be like in our terms being born in a beer case in a ghetto alley. Presently that baby grown to be the prophet of Nazareth, declared in His first message: "The Lord . . . has anointed me to preach good news to the poor . . . to proclaim release to the captives" (Luke 4:18).

There is no doubt that God is not a neutral God. Jesus reveals a stance which places him as a liberating figure among the poor and the dispossessed. To be obedient to him the Christian messenger must then surely proclaim his message with a radical accent. A radical, revolutionary Jesus is today abroad in the earth.

How, by what method, shall the prophetic element of the gospel appear in evangelism? It must be heard as of the essence of the message to be proclaimed. At one and the same time the call to personal commitment and the challenge to set about creating a just world must be heard. Christian evangelism must be there amid the contention of ideas where men and women are struggling for concepts which will show the way forward. The preacher must be present in the fashioning of a world opinion which will make poverty and injustice unendurable. He will express the conviction that to be a

Christian is to find privilege unbearable until it is shared.

Every Sunday afternoon in Sydney, a program is presented called the Lyceum Platform. Within the Lyceum Theatre, with its message carried by radio and often subsequently the press across the country, a Christian voice is declared on the great issues facing Australia and the world. This platform seeks to be the voice of the voiceless and the conscience of the people. It takes its place in the total thrust of the message and mission of a city church.

The Lyceum Platform proclaims a point of view. The church often fails by becoming merely a debating society, engaging far too often only in dialogue. The great need is for a clear declaration to be given. This means taking sides in controversial issues. This means controversy. Yet this is what we attempt in the Lyceum Platform. Speakers are not set up to cancel each other out. A Christian point of view, as found in the World Council of Churches' statements or the social pronouncements of the Methodist church, is offered. It is this clarity of proclamation which gives the Lyceum platform its strength.

Let one illustration suffice. The Australian government in 1974 set out to turn the United Nations Charter of Human Rights into an Australian covenant of human rights. A bill was presented to the Australian government which markedly diverged from the United Nations Charter. There were perils in this bill, particularly in terms of a Christian understanding of the place of the family, the rights of parents, and freedom of worship. The Lyceum Platform was held under the title "Amend the Human Rights Bill." Three speakers, a Roman

Catholic Bishop, an Episcopalian Bishop, and a Methodist minister analyzed, criticized, and offered creative suggestions concerning the bill. Great public interest was shown. The program was presented live on radio; television cameras presented the message through newscasts, and the next day the meeting was headline news in almost every newspaper in Australia. Within a few days the Columbia Broadcasting Corporation of America asked for a five-minute interview with one of the speakers on the subject. The main addresses of the afternoon were conveyed to the Australian Attorney-General who was responsible for the bill in Parliament.

Some months later, the effectiveness of the meeting was shown. A personal letter came from the Attorney-General of Australia saying that the major amendments suggested at the Lyceum meeting would be incorporated into the bill.

In today's struggle for human justice there will be occasions where talk is not enough. There will be a call for Christians to take their places in protest marches, prayer vigils, and in overt acts of nonviolence. The withdrawal of money in an attempt to put pressure on South Africa in relation to its apartheid policy can be a powerful weapon. To share fully in these ways in the struggle for righteousness is part of a vital evangelism.

The proclamation of a prophetic message in evangelism will present a new image to the world. It is also to be landed in controversy and opposition. To present a total gospel demands courage. There is a costliness about it in commitment, in tension, in the raising of antagonism in the uprooting of entrenched evil. Somehow, evangelism in these coming days must have behind it the insights and the vigor of liberation theology.

In northeastern Brazil is a Christian leader named Archbishop Camara who is a symbol in our time of the prophetic church. As a Roman Catholic Archbishop he is a man loved by the people but hated by the men of wealth in Brazil and South America. He is not prepared to proclaim a gospel that leaves society unscathed. He is not willing simply to engage in social service. As Archbishop Camara himself puts it: "If I hand out food or teach children to read, I am a saint, if I concern myself with underlying problems of reform, I am a communist." But Archbishop Camara goes on doing more than handing out food and teaching children, more than dealing with the symptoms of a sick society. He seeks in the name of a liberating God to set the people free. This is real evangelism.

POWER FOR MISSION

The greatest of all issues facing the Christian community is how to find power for mission. There is no lack of yearning for effectiveness in evangelism. There is no shortage of penetrating analysis of the church and the world. Effort—dedicated, sometimes feverish, mostly sincere—never ceases. Words flow endlessly. Yet deeply we confess it: how little appears to be achieved. Power, give us power for witness, power for mission; power for mission—this is the cry which arises amid the search for a new evangelism.

Power, spiritual power, is what the New Testament is all about. Take the first two chapters of the book of Acts. The eleven disciples assembled on the Mount of Olives around the risen Christ. They asked Jesus a question: "Lord, will you at this time restore the kingdom to Israel?" (Acts 1:6). Jesus at once points them not backwards to possible restoration, but forward in mission. He directs them to the expanding task. They were to be his witnesses in Jerusalem, Judea, Samaria, and to the ends of the earth. His promise was that a Jewish sect was to become a universal faith. They were commissioned to be his witnesses. Then came the promise: "You shall receive power when the Holy Spirit has come upon you" (Acts 1:8).

The fulfillment of the promise was delayed by only a few weeks. Soon power fell on the infant church. This is how it happened: "When the day of Pentecost had come, they were all together in one place. And suddenly a sound came from heaven like the rush of a mighty wind . . . and they were all filled with the Holy Spirit" (Acts 2:1-4).

The time is long overdue to take God seriously. That means standing in awe before his authority and power and constantly seeking a fresh vision of his face. That means searching for the power to communicate the gospel, searching for the interpreter spirit, which is the Holy Spirit. That means seeing Jesus as deliverer and recovering faith in the fact of his transforming power which can bring about the conversion of men and women. That means plunging into the struggle for righteousness, freedom, and peace with him. That means making a vocation of godliness, so that word and life woven together will be his declaration of salvation to the world.

The Fresh Vision of God

A fresh vision of God's face is the beginning of power. Only a heightened faith in what God can do will send us out in strength for mission. There is a revealing incident in the life of Jesus where his disciples asked the secret of his power. Jesus had come down from the mount of Transfiguration. At once he was confronted by a disturbed boy whom the disciples had been unable to calm. Jesus, demonstrating his power, healed the lad. Later the disciples said to Jesus, "What must we do to work the

101

works of God?" Jesus did not directly answer that activist question. He went behind action to thought, to belief. What must you do? Believe in him whom God has sent. The answer was in the realm of belief. The need of the disciples was not for more effective action, not method, but for a larger faith.

There is today a serious loss of confidence in God, in what Christ can do, in the church. As a result there is among Christians a great deal of emphasizing secondary things, such as counseling, social services, social action. All of these are a necessary part of the gospel as we have tried to declare, but they are not absolutely central, they are not the creative core of the gospel.

The Christian faith exists supremely to bring about a confrontation between God and the people. All loses vitality and is in peril of failing when the vivid realization of the presence and the power of God declines. Power for mission depends on frequently catching a fresh glimpse of God's face. Unless there are in our private lives as Christians constant new beginnings, no power will flow.

Prayer always lies at the heart of effective evangelism. I am convinced that when we cease to pray, the face of God grows dim. The cynical phrase, "God talk," has denigrated prayer. There is probably less prayer taking place in the life of Christians and in the corporate functioning of the church today than for many decades. Without prayer God does vanish into the distance.

I remember an Australian bishop, Bishop Moyes, saying that he had seen many ministers and priests resign from the Christian ministry. He said: "I've always made it a practice when a minister came to me to tell me he was pulling out of the ministry to ask the question: 'How long is it since you ceased to pray?' I have never found anyone who did not admit that for at least six months he had ceased to pray."

Prayer and power, inevitably, inextricably belong together. Spiritual drop-outs from the ministry and the laity are related to the quality of the prayer life. So if in evangelism there are to be spiritual resources there must be power in prayer, in the personal lives of those involved in mission, and in the life of the church.

God has many new resources to pour into the lives of those who trust him. We are passing through a time of difficulty and toughness in today's world. Dr. Norman Goodall says that "we are set in one of the great waiting times of Christian history." This means that there must be in all of us an inner core of passivity, of unhurried, quiet trust. This does not mean inactivity, but it does mean that as we work and witness, we wait. We wait for the Lord, who in his own good time, and when all things are ready will pour out, without measure, his power upon the church and the world.

THE INTERPRETER'S SPIRIT

Power for mission depends on discovering the gift of the Holy Spirit as an interpreter. It means finding something which will overcome the limitation so many within the Christian church feel today, which is that there is a barrier which blocks people hearing and receiving the good news of Jesus.

Jesus realized the tremendous importance of the gift of hearing. He said again and again: "He who has ears to hear, let him hear" (Matt. 11:15). Therefore, one of the great promises he made was that when the Holy Spirit came to the world he would be an interpreter; he would bring to memory things which he, Jesus, had said. He would help people to hear, to understand the gospel.

The Day of Pentecost was the fulfillment of this promise. At once on that day, a miracle of hearing was demonstrated. As Peter preached, people from many races grasped the truth. Wonderingly they said: "How is it that we hear, each of us in his own native language?" (Acts 2:8). This was the miracle, not of speaking in other tongues, but of hearing, each man in his own tongue. In other words the spirit was given to communicate the truth, to interpret the truth.

The great need today that is felt by all who speak and preach is to find power in communication. To step into a pulpit, to sit before a microphone, or peer into a television camera is to be conscious of how hard it is through words to transmit truth from mind to mind. The Holy Spirit was given as a great resource to achieve this very end. He was given to enable people to hear.

I was speaking recently in a youth gathering, and the kind of freedom came which speakers sometimes experience. The message seemed to be getting through, penetrating. One of the people suddenly said, "Your comin' through," and another one cried out, "Right on." I was thrilled; something was being heard. All who speak and preach know what this kind of satisfaction means. There are times when a message seems to vanish into the void or is like a hollow voice bouncing back from a brick wall. On other occasions there is the sense that the message is being received, absorbed by the hearers. "You are coming through" is the testimony. The Spirit is carrying out his ancient miracle in our presence; people are hearing.

To seek the power of the Spirit is part of the struggle of evangelism, new and old. Unless the Spirit of God picks up and uses that which we try to say and do, little will happen. Because of the promise of Jesus we can with confidence proclaim the good news knowing that there is available to us power in communication.

FAITH IN CONVERSION

For effective evangelism there must be faith in the transforming power of Jesus Christ, in the reality of the conversion experience. Without a conviction that the new birth, as Jesus described it, can happen, there will be no victory in the proclamation of an evangelical faith.

We are placed in an era where there is much conventional, formal religion. It is easy to see how it has developed. At a time of religious vitality people come into a vital, living personal faith. Children are born into these homes of faith but often fail to discover its reality. Yet they continue to be related to the church. In their lives are some of the fruits of the gospel transmitted by the cultural strength of a family. There is a great difference between Christians who can say "I know in whom I have believed" and those who can only comment "I know somebody who does believe." The church in its ministry can very easily, almost imperceptibly, move over to the nurture of those who are related to its life and the call for commitment, and conversion becomes muted.

In many parts of the Western World this situation has been reached today. Millions upon millions of people who bear the name Christian know little or nothing about its true inwardness in terms of power and joy. They must be won again into the full light of faith through the transforming power of Jesus Christ.

Bishop Gerald Kennedy declares that in the early days of the Circuit Riders in Methodism in America, the men who followed the Western Frontier were called the "Now Men." The name arose because in saloon bars and isolated shacks and the pioneer churches, the preacher passionately sought the conversion of men and women, shouting: "Now is the day of salvation, now is the accepted time." There was the note of urgency, of immediacy in everything they said and did.

Today many of us who present the Christian gospel deserve only the title of "gradual men." We see the Christian faith in terms of nurture, of aiding people to step onto the escalator of Christian education, which leads to church membership. Unfortunately along this route many do not come to an immediate experience of God in Christ.

The new evangelism must recover faith in conversion. Millions of people cry out for deliverance from compulsive habits such as are being created through drugs and alcohol and sexual addiction and the snares of materialism. For this very purpose Jesus came into the world. He took the name Deliverer. He came to set the captives free.

Several years ago, as President of the Methodist Church in New South Wales in Australia, I conducted a year-long campaign entitled, "Newness, New South Wales." The plan was to conduct twenty-six missions of four or eight days duration in all city and country areas. As the aim was to reach out beyond the church, to offer Christ to the people, the principle was adopted that no meetings were to be held in church buildings. This was to be the church going to the people where they were.

The first of these special missions was held in a satellite city in Sydney, called Parramatta. The meetings were held in the parking lot of a large department store. On the opening Sunday afternoon as the meeting began there was a roar of motor cycles, and a gang of twenty came into the lot. Later they told us their purpose in coming was to disturb the meeting. They did, as they stomped around talking and acting ostentatiously. However, they did remain until the end of the meeting, gradually seeming to listen to what was happening.

So began a strange relationship; each lunch hour they came into the city square, asking their questions. Each night the car park echoed to the roar of their bikes as they arrived. Friday came, youth night. When the usual call for open commitment to Jesus Christ was made I was stirred to see the leader of that gang step forward and move quietly up the aisle between the seats. Later six or eight of the gang stepped beside him at the front of the parking lot. As they bowed in prayer I was deeply moved, for I could see the name of the gang written in large letters on the back of their leather jackets: Satan's Slaves. So within the following months Satan's Slaves became Christ's men.

That is conversion!

WORKING WITH GOD

Power in mission depends on finding what God is doing in his world and doing it with him. Only as we

107

obey the will of God can we expect his power to flow. Sometimes we imagine we find God in detachment. And we do. However, the larger measure of God's strength comes as we are prepared to plunge into his world taking risks for his sake and trying to discover how we may be instruments for his purposes among the people.

There is a grand Old Testament story which tells of three young Hebrews who refused to betray their faith by idolatry. They were taken and thrown into a fiery furnace by King Nebuchadnezzar. The story says that as they suffered in the furnace a fourth figure appeared beside them. Nebuchadnezzar, looking on, was puzzled and said: "Did we not cast three men bound into the midst of the fire? . . . lo, I see four men loose . . . and the form of the fourth is like the Son of God" (KJV Dan. 3:24, 25).

It is in the struggle, it is in the furnace that the Son of God joins us. I would have to confess that in my own life it has been in moments of intensity and strain in some Christian task, in plunging in faith beyond where my reason would take me, in some heat of controversy, that Christ has joined me most vividly. I have found him more often in this way than in the moment of detachment.

In conventional evangelism there is often a deep fear of controversy. Yet if the gospel causes no disturbance of mind we are probably failing to reach the place in the furnace where men and women live. And because we are not where they are, we are not where God is. Dr. Maltby gave an answer to a poem line that reads: "Man is nearer God's heart in a garden, than anywhere else on earth." His comment was, "That is just not true unless it be the

108

Garden of Gethsemane." It is in the struggle, it is in intensity of witness that we meet Christ. Play it safe, and we will not meet God.

There was one great feature of the 1960s which did show churches prepared to be involved, committed. I can still see in imagination those marching thousands walking with Martin Luther King. There were priests and nuns, white and black, arms linked, marching to Selma. So began much of the great civil rights movement of the blacks in America.

I can remember standing near Cape Town harbor and looking out at that lonely little island where the political prisoners of the South African government are kept. I thought of the witness of Sobukwe, a local Methodist preacher, lying there and destined to stay there for the Prime Minister of South Africa had declared it so.

I think of the brave people in Eastern Germany among whom in 1958 I conducted an evangelical mission for the Methodist church. There I met young people, who as they reached out hands for a membership ticket of the church saw another card fluttering from their hand, the card which would have admitted them to a university. Yet with courage they followed the Christ.

I think of the struggle over the Vietnam War and the participation of many Christians, and the official councils of the church against a vast iniquity. There were people like the Berrigan brothers, men like William Sloane Coffin, Jr., who paid a price because they became involved in Christian protest. I think of them all, in the struggle for a just and a free world, finding God, witnessing to God in that struggle. They demonstrated the reality of the probing sentence of Dag Hammarskjöld: "In our era the road to holiness necessarily passes through the world of action."

A VOCATION OF GODLINESS

Finally, power for mission means discovering the Holy Spirit as the enabler in our own personal lives. It means paying the price in personal prayer and sacrifice. It means daring to choose a vocation of godliness.

So often we fail to state the obvious. The new evangelism, like all Christian service and witness, demands integrity, demands dedication, demands a vivid personal experience of God. Many Christians communicate little because the faith within us has become weak. Only a personal discovery of God can be communicated to others. If faith has become merely an echo of the past or from someone else, it cannot be passed to others. At last it becomes an echo of an echo and is too faint to be heard.

Personal religion is at the very heart of effective evangelism. We hesitate to declare this truth to each other as Christians because it seems to assume that we have ourselves reached a high point of commitment. However, somehow it must be said. The measure of our power in evangelism will be the measure of our own knowledge of God.

I wonder how many of us today in any sense aspire to be a man or woman of God? So many of us within the life of the churches seem to want to appear as a man of the world, a secular man, a proficient, professional man or woman. Yet there is nothing the world cries out for more than to see men and women who live near to God.

Of one fact we can be sure, if we heed this call to

110

godliness we will not face great rivalry. There is no over-supply of men and women of God in today's world. Hence there exists no greater need than people to appear who communicate by their lives the presence of God. When standards collapse as they have in our time, how can they be elevated again except by people, who by the grace of God, live superlative lives? When mankind has fallen as low as some of the corrupt and cruel men of this century, how can mankind be led upwards except by the emergence of people who live as near to God as some seem to live near to the Devil? What a vocation is open to us, and it is open to the humblest and the greatest of us—a vocation of godliness!

Lacordaire, the Frenchman once shouted, "Lord give us some saints." How shall we find a larger measure of the power of the Holy Spirit? We must want it urgently, passionately, persistently. We must be willing to wrestle as Jacob wrestled and struggled with God at the Brook Jabbok until the breaking of the day, saying, "I will not let you go, until you bless me." We must remember that the Holy Spirit does not give his richest blessings to undisciplined and unprepared minds and hearts. So we must be ready to accept the discipline of waiting, and waiting is always harder than doing. We must be willing to sacrifice, to put aside the comforts the privileges which we might think are rightfully ours. The quality of power received in our lives will be determined by the quality of the sacrifice we are prepared to make for Christ's sake, for the people's sake.

Archbishop Soderblom of Sweden never tired of holding aloft the challenge of sanctity. Many times he returned to the theme, even right up to the time of his

death. Here is the definition of a saint that he gave: "A saint is one who reveals God's might. Saints are such as who show clearly and plainly in their lives and deeds that God lives."

A saint is someone who shows by life and deed that God lives. Lord, give us some saints.